TEA IN 18TH CENTURY *America*

Kimberly K. Walters

Foreword by Lucinda Brant

Tea in 18th Century America

Copyright © 2019 by Kimberly K. Walters

All rights reserved. This book may not be reproduced in whole or in part in any form without written permission of the copyright holder.

ISBN 978-1-7337087-0-8

Published by: K. Walters at the Sign of the Gray Horse

Printed in the United States of America

Contents

Dedication i
Foreword iii
Introduction v
1   America's Love and Hate of Tea 1
2   Tea Imports to America 25
3   Social Aspects of Taking Tea 35
4   The Tea Ceremony 63
5   Tea Equipage 69
6   Receipts with or to Take with Tea 80
7   Dessert Bills Of Fare 113
8   The Tea Act, 1773, British Parliment 149
9   Measures 155
10 Cooking Terms & Definitions 158
11 Of Colours for Confectionery 170
12 Margaret Tilghman Carroll 179
Postscript to the London Gazette 195
Postscript to the Pennsylvania Gazette 204
Paintings/Illustrations 210
Acknowledgements 212
About the Author 215
Bibliography 216

Dedication

THIS book is dedicated to the memory of my mother and father, Shirley S. and John B. King, for whom I owe my own existence. It is all due to their love, patience, and encouragement in my pursuits of family history that led me to my love of living history.

I also wanted to highlight a special lady, Mrs. Margaret Tilghman Carroll, of Mount Clare in Baltimore, Maryland. I've portrayed her at her home in Baltimore, and in the Paca House & Gardens in Annapolis, Maryland. Fascinated by her life, I have dedicated a chapter in this book to her. She left an "account book" with her niece who was the daughter to one of General George Washington's Aide de Camp, Tench Tilghman. The book has survived and is housed in the Maryland Historical Society. Within were also written down the equipage Mrs. Carroll used for tea as well as recipes of which I have included some in this book. It is with special thanks to Mount Clare Museum House for allowing me to use her portrait within her chapter as well as to the Maryland Historical Society for highlighting me in their Summer 2017 magazine.

Foreword

As the author of Georgian Historical mysteries and romances, who spends her days immersed in the eighteenth century, tea is never far from my mind. There are characters who sip tea in elegant drawing rooms over gossip and political machinations, their tea equipage proudly on display (for it was a clear indicator of status as well as wealth), while below stairs their servants are recycling the tea leaves to sell on the black market. And while my expertise is England and France in the 1700s, I am well aware of the importance of tea to the American Colonies, having taught the history of the American Revolutionary War to high school students, who are instantly fascinated when I mention a certain tea party that took place in Boston harbor.

I met Kimberly Walters online through our mutual interest in all things 18th century. As a living historian, author of a fascinating book on 18th century cookery, and a creator of beautiful and authentic 18th century reproduction jewelry, Kimberly is well suited to writing about the important role tea played in the lives — social, political and economic — of the American colonists.

Kimberly has delved deep into newspapers, diaries, pamphlets, probate lists, and letters from the time, so that this book is full to the brim with primary sources. We hear in their own words from the colonists as to their relationship with tea, and how their lives were shaped by it. There are fascinating firsthand accounts from travelers, preachers, politicians,

Tea in 18th Century America

society ladies, military men, but to name a few. All were affected in some way by this seemingly innocuous beverage.

There is also an extensive receipts section providing readers with the opportunity to plunge into creating authentic side dishes to accompany drinking their preferred type of tea in the 18th century manner.

It is with great pleasure I recommend to you Taking Tea in the 18th Century. Anyone with an interest in the history and lives of the American Colonies cannot but be intrigued and fascinated by the part played by this most satisfying beverage.

Lucinda Brant
New York Times and USA Today bestselling author of award-winning Georgian Historical Romances and Mysteries

Introduction

Tea didn't always come in a tea bag.

In 1716, Joseph Pitton de Tournefort described tea in his book, Materia Medica; or, a description of simple medicines generally us'd in physick: ... demonstrating their uses, ... also their operating ... upon human bodies ... With an appendix, shewing the nature and use of mineral waters ... as —

> "Tea of the Chinese or Jappanese of Brechmius as a Schrub growing in Japan and China, with a multitude of branches growing very thick and close; The leaves are of a dark green Colour, an inch long, half an inch broad, bitterish, and smelling of Violets: The flowers are Rosie, consisting of five whitish or pale leaves, the middle whereof is possessed with a numerous train of Chieves or Small Threads: The Pointal is chang'd into a spherical fruit, but sometimes longish, consisting of three distinct seed-vessels, and sometimes having but one: The Seeds are hard, not much unlike a Filbert nut, being of a brown Colour, and smooth, containing a Kernel that is white and wrinkled, being first of a sweetish Taste, but after turning bitter and nauseous. Tea is supposed to conduct not a little to the restoring a lost or dejected Appetite, and to the easing and removing violent Paints of the Head. Some leaves of Tea are

thrown into [3x or 3xij] of Boiling Water, and the Pot being taken from the Fire, and a little Sugar added, The Tineture or hot Liquor is drunk off by sipping; and this is commonly called Tea."

In 1995, I was on vacation in London, England. As most people do, I was looking for gifts, and purchased *The East India Book of Tea* by Anthony Wild for my father. Tea was his absolute favorite drink, and I would send him boxes from the many countries I visited while living overseas. When I was little, my father and I would often enjoy a cup together while he told me stories or we read books together. I cannot tell you how many times I asked him to read Cinderella to me! It didn't matter if it was iced or hot tea, he always had a cup within easy reach.

In fact, my mother was from New York, and my father grew up in Georgia. So, we had two types of tea served in the house — sweet (as the south loves) and unsweet (as many in the north drink). My Mom would keep our empty gallon milk jugs and reuse them to make tea. The sweet tea was for Dad, the unsweet for the rest of us, but I often sneaked some of the sweet. I grew up drinking and liking both varieties.

Introduction

After I left home in my late teens, my Dad and I would often talk on the telephone about what book he had checked out of the library as he was an avid reader or as he liked to be called, a "Bibliophile."

My father is the one that introduced me to genealogy and my family history, and that led to me researching where I came from. I then decided to join the Daughters of the American Revolution as my family links to those involved in fighting that war. The DAR gave me the introduction to others that also participated in living history, which led to new friends, my horses, and the love of dressing up 18th century.

A lot has been written about tea in books and articles. This book is focused on pulling all the relevant bits together with an emphasis on tea in 18th century America. I hope it will give you an understanding of the important, even essential, part that tea played in those days, and may this book serve you in being able to create and have an authentic tea party at home for friends and family. Several chapters in this book are also part of my book *A Book of Cookery, by a Lady* (Ingram, 2014).

As a genealogist and reenactor, I find the most rewarding research and reliable evidence comes from primary sources. To that end, I have endeavored to include as much primary source material as is fitting, so that you hear the authentic voice of the time. It is my hope that you will find much to enjoy — over a cup of most excellent tea!

CHAPTER 1

America's Love and Hate of Tea

We cannot start this book without a little history of how tea came into America. According to the British Library's records, in 1672, the English East India Company secured a trading post in Taiwan. The Company was in direct and regular trade with the Chinese from that base and was permitted to make regular voyages to Amoy, Chusan and Canton. Rodris Roth, in her pamphlet, "Tea Drinking in the 18th Century America: Its Etiquette and Equipage" says that "Tea had long been known and used in the Orient before it was introduced into Europe in the early part of the 17th century. At about the same time two other new beverages were available as well, chocolate from the

1

Americas and coffee from the Near East. The presence of these commodities in European markets is indicative of the vigorous exploration and active trade of that century, which also witnessed the successful settlement of colonies in North America. By about mid-17th century the new beverages were being drunk in England, and by the 1690's were being sold in New England. At first chocolate was preferred, but coffee, being somewhat cheaper, soon replaced it and in England gave rise to a number of public places of refreshment known as coffee houses."

Coffee was, of course, the primary drink of these establishments, but tea was available as indicated by an advertisement that appeared in an English newspaper in 1658 noted as one of the earliest advertisements for tea —

> "That Excellent, and by all Physicians approved, China Drink, called by the Chineans, Tcha, by other nations Tay alias Tee, is sold at the Sultaness-head, a Cophee-house in Sweetings Rents by The Royal Exchange, London."

In *A Voyage Round the World during the Years 1835, 1836, 1837,* Ruschenberger writes that "The highest quality of green tea is Gunpowder. This consists of the first leaves of the vernal crop of the green tea plant. As it comes to us, it is not mixed with the flowers of any foreign plant, as Peko is; but such is the case with some of the finest green teas imported by the Russians, called Chulan, Imperial, and Hyson, and Young Hyson, compose the second and third crops. The light and inferior leaves separated from Hyson by a winnowing machine, constitute Hyson Skin. The fourth and last crop constitutes Twankay, Singlo, &c. With respect to the last word, the same observation applies to it, as to Bohea. Singlo, or more correctly Songlo, takes its title from a mountain of that name in the province of Kiangnan, where the finest green tea has been long produced."

He continues, "The highest quality of black tea is Peko, or more correctly Flowery Peco. This consists of the early spring buds of the finest black tea plants, intermixed as is commonly believed, with the flowers of the fragrant olive, which is discoverable in the form of small white particles... The lowest Boheas of the Canton market consist of the refuse or sweepings of superior black teas, or of the inferior tea of Woping, in Canton. It may be remarked, by the way, respecting this word Bohea, which is now applied by Europeans to the lowest demonstration of black tea, that it was, and still is, applied by the Chinese to the finest description of it, that which grows on the mountain Vu-i-shan, in the province of Fokien, as noted for its production of fine teas as the estate of Clos-Vougeot, for its Burgundy, or that of the Chateau-Margot for its claret."

For a time, tea was esteemed mainly for its curative powers, which explains why it was "by all Physicians approved." According to an English broadside published in 1660, the numerous contemporary ailments which tea "helpeth" included "the headaches, giddiness, and heaviness."

It was also considered "good for colds, dropsies and scurvies and [it] expelleth infection. It prevents and cures agues, surfeits and fevers." By the end of the 17th century, however, tea's medicinal qualities had become secondary to its fashionableness as a unique drink. Tea along with the other exotic and novel imports from the Orient such as fragile porcelains, lustrous silks, and painted wallpapers had captured the European imagination. Though the beverage was served in public pleasure gardens as well as coffee houses during the early 1700's in England, social tea drinking in the home was gradually coming into favor. The coffee houses continued as centers of political, social, and literary influence as well as of commercial life into the first half of the 19th century, for apparently Englishmen preferred to drink their coffee in public rather than private houses and among male rather than mixed company. This was in contrast to tea, which was drunk in the home with breakfast or as a morning beverage and socially at afternoon gatherings of both sexes... As tea drinking in the home became fashionable, both host and hostess took pride in a well-appointed tea table, for a teapot of silver or fragile blue-and-white Oriental porcelain with matching cups and saucers and other equipage added prestige as well as elegance to the teatime ritual."

In 1730, Doctor Thomas Short publishes "*A Dissertation on Tea, Explaining its Properties By Many New Experiments; and Demonstrating from Philosophical Principles, the various EFFECTS it has on different Constitutions To Which is Added The Natural History of Tea…*" The history of tea is also described in more detail, and shows how much tea was beloved early in the century. There is also an appendix that discusses sage and water and compares sage with the various types of tea. Dr. Short states in his introduction that "Japan, China, and Siam are the only Places which afford us Tea…being usually of a finer clear Green, having a smaller leaf." He also says that tea was brought into the realm during the reign of James I, yet wasn't popular until the importation of large quantities by the Government. There were also two types of tea imported, Green and Bohea. Of Bohea, he describes the three types as Pekoe, Congo, and Common Bohea. Of the Green tea, he defines them as Hysson, Imperial Common, Ordinary, and Dutch Bloom. He also states that tea must be infused versus just boiled over a fire.

Newspapers in the 1740s through the 1760s in Pennsylvania, Maryland, and Virginia advertise the latest imports of tea, tea kettles, and other items for the colonists. It is interesting to note that they were also selling tea for ready money or credit. Charles Willing advertised his taking leave of the colonies back to England in the ship Macclesfield on 21 June 1750, and states that he is selling some "best singlo tea" among other items.

Printed in the Pennsylvania Gazette on 25 March 1742, is an account of Benjamin Lay, on the vanity of tea drinking.

> "On Monday about Noon, being in the Time of the General Meeting of Friends, Benjamin Lay, the Pythagorean-cynical-christian Philosopher, bore a publick Testimony against the Vanity of Tea-drinking, by devoting to Destruction in the Market-place, a large Parcel of valuable China, &c. belonging

to his deceased Wife. He mounted a Stall on which he had placed the Box of Ware; and when the People were gather'd round him, began to break it peacemeal with a Hammer; but was interrupted by the Populace, who overthrew him and his Box, to the Ground, and scrambling for the Sacrifice, carry'd off as much of it whole as they could get. Several would have purchas'd the China of him before he attempted to destroy it, but he refused to take any Price for it."

Tea equipment and furniture was sought after and became valuable. On 28 February 1755, the Virginia Gazette in Williamsburg reported that two servants stole a tea board when they left. A tea board is a tray that would have held the tea equipage, often described as being made of Mahogany. It is interesting to read about them, especially their physical descriptions. I wonder if they would have ever thought that future generations would be reading about what they did. Since I also love horses, it was interesting to read that they stole two of them as well!

"RAN away from the Subscriber, living in Spotsylvania County, on Friday the 31st of January last, Two Servants, viz. Richard Finch, about 5 Feet 6 Inches high, of a brown Complexion, with short black Hair; had on when he went away, a blue Coat with Metal Buttons, and Breeches of the same, also a brown Cloth Wastecoat; he likewise carried with him two Horses, one a bright Bay, with a small Star in his Forehead, had been lately trimm'd, and has a short Switch Tail, but no Brand to be perceived, about 14 Hands high, and paces well; the other a light Grey, about 13 Hands and a Half high, branded on the near Buttock with three Dots, half his Mane cut; both Horses shod before: He also carried from Williamsburg one Tea Board, two Waiters, three Pair of Boys Shoes, three Girls ditto, onf [sic] Damask, one Callimanco, and the other red

Leather, one Looking-Glass, one Pound Ten, and a new Saddle and Bridle. Comfort Finch, of a fair Complexion. Whoever will bring the said Servants and Horses, and other Things, to the Subscriber, shall receive two Pistoles Reward, paid by Dorothea Benger."

The love of tea did not necessarily stay that way among the colonists when in 1767 the Townshend Acts passed in England imposed a duty that included glass, lead, paper, and tea. Those in the colonies became angry by these acts as they were taxed on these items. They decided to start to protest the taxes imposed especially regarding tea. As part of the protest, some decided NOT to drink the tea which over time affected the owners of the ship cargo, and eventually the shop owner's livelihoods.

Not everyone, however, was as enthusiastic about drinking the beverage. Peter Kalm wrote in his book, *Travels Into North America: Containing Its Natural History ... with the Civil, Ecclesiastical and Commercial State of the Country* in 1771 —

> "Tea is differently esteemed by different people; and I think we would be as well, and our purses much better, if we were both without tea and coffee. However, I must be impartial, and mention in praise of tea, that if it be useful, it must certainly be so in summer, on such journeys as mine, through a desert country, where one cannot carry wine or other liquors, and where the water is generally unfit for use, as being full of insects. In such cases, it is very relishing when boiled, and tea is drunk with it; and

I cannot sufficiently describe the fine taste it has in such circumstances. It relieves a weary traveller more than can be imagined, as I have myself experienced, together with a great many others who have travelled through the desert forests of America; on such journeys, tea is found to be almost as necessary as victuals."

The colonists already had a hard time with The Stamp Act; however, when The Tea Act was passed by Parliament on May 10, 1773, it was the final straw that led to the rebellion in Boston. I have included the act as a later chapter so that you can read it for yourself. Some understanding of what was going on in politics of the day need also be known.

The act was not intended to raise revenue in the American colonies, and in fact imposed no new taxes. It was designed to prop up the East India Company which was foundering financially and burdened with 18 million pounds of unsold tea. This tea was to be shipped directly to the colonies, and sold at a bargain price, but unfortunately, the Townshend Duties were still in place. Those in America found reason to believe that the Tea Act was a maneuver to buy popular support for the taxes already in place. The direct sale of tea, via British agents, would also undercut the business of local merchants. This wasn't taken well, and is described better within a Postscript to the Pennsylvania Gazette on a Friday Evening at Five 'Clock, December 24, 1773 within Philadelphia (found later in this book). It is better to read from the reporting of the day what took place in Boston regarding the reason for dumping the tea, and for what we now know as the "Boston Tea Party."

By January 20, 1774 Virginia Gazette, a poem was printed, author unknown, that proliferated through the colonies as an expression of the renouncement of tea in rhyme form. It also provides a wonderful picture of contemporary teatime etiquette and equipage.

A Lady's Adieu to Her Tea-Table

FAREWELL the Tea-board with your gaudy attire,
Ye cups and ye saucers that I did admire;
To my cream pot and tongs I now bid adieu;
That pleasure's all fled that I once found in you.
Farewell pretty chest that so lately did shine,
With hyson and congo and best double fine;
Many a sweet moment by you I have sat,
Hearing girls and old maids to tattle and chat;
And the spruce coxcomb laugh at nothing at all,
Only some silly work that might happen to fall.
No more shall my teapot so generous be
In filling the cups with this pernicious tea,
For I'll fill it with water and drink out the same,
Before I'll lose LIBERTY that dearest name,
Because I am taught (and believe it is fact)
That our ruin is aimed at in the late act,
Of imposing a duty on all foreign Teas,
Which detestable stuff we can quit when we please.
LIBERTY'S The Goddess that I do adore,
And I'll maintain her right until my last hour,
Before she shall part I will die in the cause,
For I'll never be govern'd by tyranny's laws.

There were other articles written about what took place in Boston that is included in the chapter on the act itself. It is definitely worth understanding the mindset of those in England on what took place in Boston.

As word got out and things escalated, we start to see up and down the colonies what people thought of the issue. John Adams wrote to his wife, Abagail, while he was in Boston on May 12, 1774 that he was still drinking tea while he was away. We do not know if he was drinking imported China tea or a medicinal tea. He wrote, —

> "…I am unwearied in my Endeavours to subdue it, and have the Pleasure to think I have had some Success. I rise at 5, walk 3 Miles, keep the Air all day and walk again in the Afternoon. These Walks have done me more good than any Thing — tho I have had constantly plied with Teas, and your Specific. My own Infirmities, the Account of the Return of yours and the public News, coming altogether have put my Utmost Phylosophy to the Tryal..."

But by May of 1774, the Virginia House of Burgesses met to discuss the tax on tea and the act further imposed upon them. The *Virginia Gazette* reported on May 27, 1774 —

> "This Day, at ten o'Clock, the Honourable Members of the late House of Burgesses met, by Agreement, at the long Room in the Raleigh Tavern, in this City, called the Apollo," where an "Agreement was unanimously entered into by that patriotick Assembly, in Support of the constitutional Liberties of AMERICA, against the late oppressive Act of the British Parliament respecting the Town of Boston, which, in the End, must affect all the other Colonies." (Va. Gaz., P&D, 26 May 1774) The meeting agreed to boycott tea and other goods of the East India Company. They then directed their committee of correspondence to write to other colonies "on the expediency of appointing deputies from the several colonies of British America, to meet in general congress." George Washington joined the other burgesses and a number of local leaders in signing the statement.

> **Written by a LADY, on receiving a handsome Set of TEA CHINA.**
>
> SPECIOUS Instrument of Ill,
> Banish'd, in Disgrace retire;
> Let Concealment hide thee still,
> Nor to publick View aspire.
>
> You indeed, in Days of Yore,
> Would have met a better Fate;
> Plac'd amidst my choicest Store,
> Serv'd for Use or serv'd for State.
>
> Still, alas! thou migh'ft have been
> Chiefest Favourite of the Fair;
> Now thou art with Horrour seen
> As a ministerial Snare.
>
> Dar'dst thou hope thy gaudy Dress
> (Soldier's like) of Gold and Blue,
> E'er could make thy Guilt the less,
> Or my steady Soul subdue.
>
> Know! the Luxuries of Life
> One by one I can resign;
> But, thou, Volunteer in Strife,
> India, first farewel to thine.

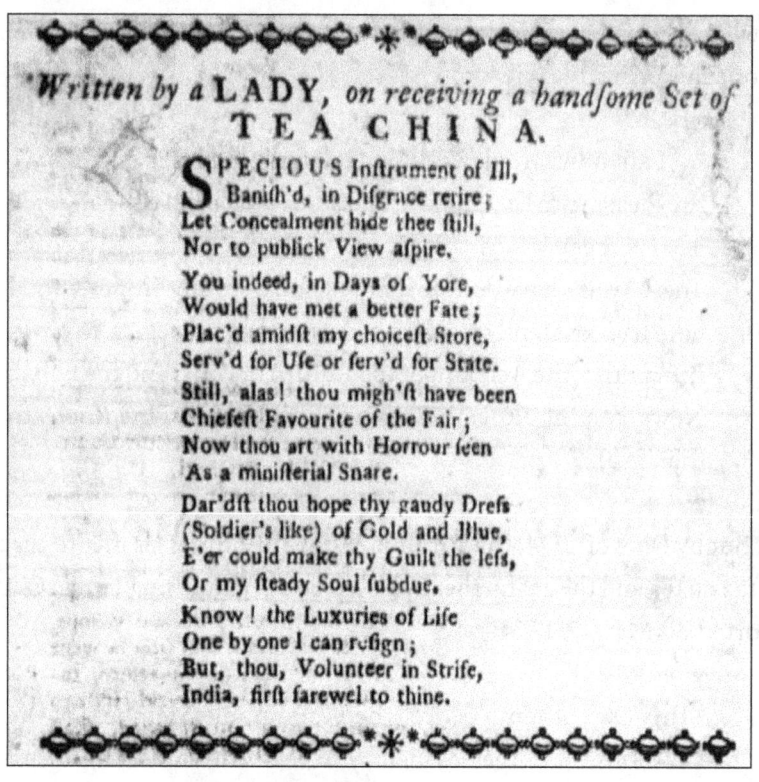

The Virginia Gazette, June 16, 1774

We start to see the progression of entire towns deciding to come together to support Boston. Tiverton, in the Massachusetts Colony, on June 16, 1774 was reported in the Virginia Gazette to have "left off drinking Tea, a glorious Example!"

Another letter from John Adams to his wife on July 4, 1774, in a post script mentions, "I believe I forgot to tell you one Anecdote: When I first came to this House it was late in the afternoon, and I had ridden 35 miles at least. "Madam" said I to Mrs. Huston, "it is lawfull for a weary Traveller to refresh himself with a Dish of Tea provided it has been honestly Smuggled, or paid no Duties." "No, sir," said she, we have renounced all Tea in this Place. I can't make Tea, but I'll make you

Coffee." Accordingly I have drank Coffee every afternoon since, and have borne it very well. Tea must be universally renounced. I must be weaked, and the sooner, the better."

In Virginia, Bryan Fairfax writes to George Washington on August 5, 1774 and considers why this beverage of tea was refused and boycotted, "...When the Duty on Tea was laid as an external Duty we objected to it, and with some Reason, because it was not for the regulation of Trade, but for the express purpose of raising a Revenue..." in which to bail out a company in debt to the crown. (GW Papers at the Library of Congress)

The Committee of Correspondence of Fairfax County, Virginia, PORTBO. Augst. 9th. 1774, says,

> "GENT. We are just informed of the Arrival of the Brige Mary & Jane Capt. Chapman from London with a large Quantity of Tea destined for Norfolk and Consigned to Neil Jamisson & Co. Geo & Jno. Bowness & Jno Laurence & Co.--The Brige. now lyes in Wecomicoe River in Maryland and we are informed will either sail to Norfolk & deliver the Tea or it will be sent in small Craft from where the Vessell now lyes. There is also a Quantity of Tea on board the above Vessell for several Gent on Potomack River, particularly Geo Town Bladensburgh, Chapticoe & Leonard Town and this place. We think it our duty to prevent any of it being Landed here & for that end have this day called a meeting; We think it not only our duty to obstruct its being Landed here, but also to Afford our Friends an opportunity of doing the same if they chuse to join in frustrating the destructive plan which seems to have been laid by the Consigners of that detestable Article, And for that purpose we have given information to George Town, Bladensburgh & Piscattaway & forwarded dispatches to Norfolk--And that you may be guarded be pleased to receive this intelligence from ... Gent ... Yr most Ob Servts.

> ... THE COMMITTEE OF CHARLES COUNTY it is imagined there will be an Attempt to Land it at Dumfries or Allexa. privately if they find they cannot do it in Maryland. A note was written upon the back of this letter: "Mr Clifford Be pleased to send your Boat over to Alexandria with this Letter, immediately on receit of it, with instructions to your people to deliver it into the hands of Mr Ro. Harrison, & you will very much Oblige Yr most Obt Servt. R Hooe."

The Pennsylvania Packet introduced a letter on September 26, 1774, from a young man that went to the East Indies to find tea to bring back to the colonies to grow. The Packet writes, "The following extract of a letter just arrived from a young gentleman formerly of this city, now settled in the East-Indies, is of so interesting a nature that I am satisfied it must give great pleasure to every American, as the tea seeds therein mentioned, are come over in good order, and are distributed among some very curious gardeners. Should we be happy enough to raise the tea plant on this continent, the East India Company may rue the day they lent their aid to the Ministry to enslave the Americans."

On October 17, 1774, the Pennsylvania Journal published an article, by order of the Congress sitting in Philadelphia, of "THE Resolutions" entered into by the Delegates from the several towns and districts in the county of Suffolk, in the province of Massachusetts-Bay, on Tuesday the 6th inst. and their Address to his Excellency Governor Gage, dated the 9th instant, as laid before Congress. It is a long and lengthy article, but it has several resolves in which number 14 stated —

> "That until our rights are fully restored to us, we will, to the utmost of our power, and recommend the same to the other counties, withhold all commercial intercourse with Great-Britain, Ireland, and the West-Indies, and abstain from the consumption of British merchandize and manufactures,

and especially of East-India Teas and piece good, with such additions, alterations, and exceptions only, at the Grand Congress of the colonies may agree to."

This starts the open and written dissatisfaction of those in the colonies and the Crown with the taxes that started after the French and Indian war. Their resolution started with,

"WHEREAS the power, but not the justice; the vengeance, but the wisdom of Great-Britain, which of old persecuted, scourged, and excited our fugitive Parents from their native shores, now pursues us, their guiltless children, with unrelenting severity: And whereas, this then savage and uncultivated desart was purchased by the toil our venerable progenitors, to us they belour of those our venerable progenitors, to us they bequeathed the dear bought inheritance, to our care and protection they consigned it, and the most sacred obligations are upon us to transmit the glorious purchase, unfettered by power, unclogged with shackle, to our innocent and beloved offspring..."

The Association signed by the Ladies of Edenton, North Carolina, on October 25, 1774 were resolved not to drink tea in solidarity with much of the rest of the colonies — in the Morning Chronicle and London Advertiser of January 16, 1775 — an article in the paper said, —

"Edenton, North Carolina, Oct 17, 1774
The Provincial Deputies of North Carolina having resolvd not to drink any more tea, nor wear any more British cloth, &c. many ladies of this Province have determined to give a memorable proof of their patriotism, and have accordingly entered into the following honourable and spirited association. I send

it to you, to shew your fair countrywomen, how zealously and faithfully American ladies follow the laudable example of their husbands, and what opposition your Ministers may expect to receive from a people thus firmly united against them."

A clipping of the original paper, with the ladies resolution are as follows along with the names of all of the ladies that signed it.

> "*Edenton, North Carolina*, Oct. 25,
>
> "As we cannot be indifferent on any occasion that appears nearly to affect the peace and happiness of our country, and as it has been thought necessary, for the public good, to enter into several particular resolves by a meeting of members deputed from the whole Province, it is a duty which we owe, not only to our near and dear connections, who have concurred in them, but to ourselves, who are essentially interested in their welfare, to do every thing as far as lies in our power, to testify our sincere adherence to the same; and we do therefore accordingly subscribe this paper, as a witness of our fixed intention and solemn determination to do so.
>
> | | |
> |---|---|
> | Abigail Charlton | Mary Blount |
> | F. Johnstone | Elizabeth Creacy |
> | Margaret Cathcart | Elizabeth Patterson |
> | Anne Johnstone | Jane Wellwood |
> | Margaret Pearson | Mary Woolard |
> | Penelope Dawson | Sarah Beasley |
> | Jean Blair | Susannah Vail |
> | Grace Clayton | Elizabeth Veil |
> | Frances Hall | Elizabeth Vail |
> | Mary Jones | Mary Creacy |
> | Anne Hall | Mary Creacy |
> | Rebecca Bondfield | Ruth Benbury |
> | Sarah Littlejohn | Sarah Howcott |
> | Penelope Barker | Sarah Hoskins |
> | Elizabeth P. Ormond | Mary Littledle |
> | M. Payne | Sarah Vallentine |
> | Elizabeth Johnston | Elizabeth Crickett |
> | Mary Bonner | Elizabeth Green |
> | Lydia Bonner | Mary Ramsey |
> | Sarah Howe | Anne Horniblow |
> | Lydia Bennet | Mary Hunter |
> | Marion Wells | Tresia Cunningham |
> | Anne Anderson | Elizabeth Roberts |
> | Sarah Mathews | Elizabeth Roberts |
> | Anne Haughton | Elizabeth Roberts." |
> | Elizabeth Beasley | |

This resolution produced a response in the mother country. The following is a January 31, 1775 letter from Arthur Iredell in London (Queen Square) to his brother James (who was in Edenton). James Iredell was married to Hannah Johnston, whose brother Samuel was a wealthy landowner and her sister, Elizabeth, was one of the signers of the Edenton pledge. James was appointed a collector of the customs for the Port of Roanoke in Edenton at the time and wrote "To the Inhabitants of Great Britain," opposing the concept of Parliamentary supremacy over America among other things. His mindset seems to have also carried over to his wife Hannah, but his brother Arthur was not happy with the resolves. In a letter Arthur writes —

"Dear Brother: I see by the newspaper the Edenton ladies have signalized themselves by their protest against tea drinking. The name of Johnston I see among others; are any of my sister's relations patriotic heroines? Is there a female congress at Edenton too? I hope not, for we Englishmen are afraid of the male congress, but if the ladies, who have ever since the Amazonian era been esteemed the most formidable enemies; if they, I say, should attack us, the most fatal consequence is to be dreaded. So dexterous in the handling of a dart, each wound they give is mortal; whilst we, so unhappily formed by nature, the more we strive to conquer them, the more we are conquered. The Edenton ladies, conscious, I suppose, of this superiority on their side, by a former experience, are willing I imagine, to crush us into atoms by their omnipotency; the only security on our side to prevent the impending ruin, that I can preceive [sic], is the probability that there are but few places in America which possess so much female artillery as Edenton. Pray let me know all the particulars when you favor me with a letter. Your most affectionate friend and brother. ARTHUR IREDELL."

Arthur wrote again to his brother, James, on 27 April 1775 from London and midway through the letter, he asks him "...How does Charles do? Remember me most affectionately to Him. Often do I transport myself to Edenton (I was going to say, and drink a dish of Tea with you, but I recollected myself time enough to prevent my putting so great a disgrace upon You) and seat myself in the midst of you all. When Shall We all compose so happy a Circle?" It seems that he was being sarcastic while asking about their brother (Charles).

It is interesting how things progress and are reported within the papers. I wanted to capture as much as I could about both sides.

The Virginia Gazette published on May 11, 1775, that "They write from New York, that a surprising progress continues to be made, both there and at Philadelphia, in the establishment of manufactures, by means of experienced artificers from Great Britain and Ireland. Most of the Ladies in America, after the manner of the Roman females, are sending their jewels to Philadelphia, there to remain till May, when the Congress meet, who are to have the disposal of them, if necessity requires it, for the glorious cause of liberty; and farther declared, that if their persons should be wanted, they will fearless take the field against their enemies." While this isn't specifically about tea, it continues the mindset of the wrongs perceived and brought by the King, and the concerted effort to get what they believe they deserve — liberty, justice, and the freedom in which to live as they will so far away. This is also published about a month into what is the American War of Independence and shortly after the battles of Lexington and Concord.

Yet, there are some still "taking tea" with guests during the war. Quaker Sally Wister describes in her journal having tea on October 26, 1777 with a Dr. Diggs that she says is a "very disagreeable man." Sally lived in Phildelphia and had to flee after the war intensified. There are many instances of her sitting down to tea with guests and family, and even the man that asked her to marry him. She does not describe what type of tea they drink, but still performed the ceremony none-the-less.

America's Love and Hate of Tea

In August of 1779, Barnaby Owning reported that "five teaspoons, one marked S.P.A., and four marked W.S." were stolen out of his house while he was living on Haddonfield Road. He offered "Eighty dollars" reward they were that valuable to him.

During the war, it also seems that at Head Quarters in West Point on September 24, 1779, a letter was written stating that tea would be given as a dividend —

> "Dear Sir: I am favd. with yours of the 22d. ... The quantity of Cloathing issued in July, under the General order, was so very trifling, that it would not have extended to any thing like the supply of the Officers of the whole Army. They therefore who first applied were first served, by which means a vast number on the spot, were put in the same situation with the officers of your Regt. There is at this time a small dividend of Tea and pepper to be made, of which Genl. Howe has been advised, and of which the Officers under his command will I presume take the advantage." (GW Papers)

In this instance, 12 silver teaspoons were stolen in 1780. The Virginia Gazette reported on July 19 that, "FIVE HUNDRED DOLLARS REWARD FOR taking up BAKER HAZARD, a mulatto man, almost white, about 5 feet 8 inches high, pitted with the smallpox, was born in Virginia (where he is now supposed to be) and waited on Mr. Gill of the Maryland regiment of light dragoons until he was taken prisoner last summer, and may probably endeavour to pass as his servant still. He took from me, when he went away, two bay horses, and 6000 dollars in loan office certificates (not filled up) of 1000 each, signed Francis Hopkins, treasurer of loans, and countersigned William Gibbs, a dozen silver tea spoons, and a pair of silver shoe buckles; had on when he run away from Hillsborough in North Carolina, a brown coat turned up with green, and dark brown horseman's cloak, with a red cape. Whoever takes up and secures the said fellow, shall receive the above reward, and reasonable charges paid by ANTHONY W. WHITE. COL. 1st R.L.D."

Four dollars reward was offered and advertised in the Pennsylvania Packet in Philadelphia for a tea urn that had been stolen — it was a "new fashioned Tea Urn without a heater, spout, handles, feet, and small urn at the top of the cover plate." It was stolen out of the front parlour of the owner on Third Street." "Without the heater" possibly meant there was not a stand underneath to put coals or flame to keep it warm.

While many believe that tea was not available during the time of the American War for Independence, it is noted on several occasions from orders within Annapolis to London or even within George Washington's account of expenses on November 1, 1781, that tea was purchased. In the case of George Washington, John Likley, a Philadelphia merchant sold the army tea as they passed through that city in September of that year. However, the type of tea was not described. (GW Papers at the Library of Congress)

Alexander Hamilton wrote to Jeremiah Wadsworth, from New Windsor, New York that he needed "a pound of good green tea" on April 16, 1781—

> Dr Sir,
>
> As I intend in a day or two to take lodgings for Mrs. Hamilton, I take the liberty to request you will do me the favour to procure and send me by the earliest opportunity a pound of good green tea & a dozen knives and forks such as you purchased for Mrs. Jacob Cuyler at Albany, for which I will thankfully send you the cost by the first conveyance.
>
> I am Dr. Sir truly   Yr. friend & servant
> A Hamilton
> The expresses may take charge of them.
> Hd. Qrs. April 16th.

After the War

After the American War for Independence, the tea ceremony continued. As the new nation was being formed and imports started to flow back into the colonies, since they were free from any acts or decrees of the British Crown, they would be able to import what they wished and it would not have to go to England before it hit the new American shores.

In October of 1786, Thomas Jefferson wrote to his daughter, Martha Jefferson, that they would have tea —

> "To Martha Jefferson
> [Oct. 1786]
>
> I will call for you today, my dear between twelve and one. You must be dressed, because we drink tea with Mrs. Montgomery. Bring your music and drawings. Adieu my dear Patsy."
> (Founders, http://founders.archives.gov/documents/Jefferson/01-10-02-0351)

Even during a ceremony on the anniversary of independence, on July 9, 1788, a celebration was reported in The Pennsylvania Packet in Elizabethtown, Pennsylvania. The gentleman of the Cincinnati convened at the convivial board...After a military parade, they gave 13 toasts and each was "attended with the discharge of cannon, and an eau de joy from the troops ended the day." The next day, an assembly of ladies added a "double lustre to the rejoicings, by honoring the gentleman with their presence at the bower, where the company was served, tea, cake wine, &tc., accompanied by music." It seems that this was a three day celebration!

A DISH of TEA.

In Imitation of Philip's Manner.

PRETTY charmer, glossy dish,
  Daily object of my wish,
Let me sip the liquid Tea,
Liquid leaf from India tree!
How I feel my spirits flow,
And new vigour in me glow,
When from Tea-pot you distil,
Little Tea-pot's smoaking rill;
And you lose your golden stream
In a silver flood of cream;
And I lift you to my lip,
And, like nectar, thee I sip;
Oh! how charming in the bliss
Of thy aromatic kiss!

Happy he, who twice a day
Thus can taste his life away,
Who with each returning morn
After walking o'er the lawn,
And at night again can sip
India fragrance from thy lip,
Purer joys by far he knows,
Than those which from Bacchus flows;
Fit for who's a flame of mine,
Fit for Chloe, maid divine!

The Pennsylvania Packet, 23 December 1788

William Priest, Musician, late of the Theatres Philadelphia, Baltimore, and Boston, wrote of his travels in a journal from 1793 to 1797. He writes an excellent description that Americans are drinking tea throughout the day.

"Philadelphia, March 7th, 1794.

DEAR SIR,

It is a general observation with respect to the English, that they eat more animal food than the people of any other nation. The following statement of the manner of living of the Americans [Footnote: By the term American you must understand a white man descended from a native of the Old Continent; and by the term Indian, or Savage, one of the aborigines of the New World.] will convince you of the falsity of this opinion.

About eight or nine in the morning they breakfast on tea and coffee, attended always with what they call relishes, such as salt fish, beef-steaks, sausages, broiled-fowls, ham, bacon, &c. At two they dine on what is usual in England, with a variety of american dishes, such as bear, opossum, racoon, &c. At six or seven in the evening they have their supper, which is exactly the same as their breakfast, with the addition of what cold meat is left at dinner. I have often wondered how they acquired this method of living, which is by no means calculated for the climate; such stimulating food at breakfast and supper naturally causes thirst, and there being no other beverage at these meals than tea, or coffee, they are apt to drink too freely of them, particularly the female part of the family; which, during the excessive heats in summer, is relaxing and debilitating; and in winter, by opening the pores, exposes them to colds of the most dangerous kind.

The manner of living I have been describing is that of people in moderate circumstances; but this taste for relishes with coffee and tea extends to all ranks of people in these states. Soon after my arrival at this city, I went on a party of pleasure to a sort of tea-garden and tavern [Footnote: By the word tavern, in America, is meant an inn or public house of any description.], romantically situate on the bank of the Scuylkill. At six in the evening we ordered coffee, which I was informed they were here famous for serving in style. I took a memorandum of what was on the table; viz. coffee, cheese, sweet cakes, hung beef, sugar, pickled salmon, butter, crackers, ham, cream, and bread. The ladies all declared, it was a most charming relish!

Yours sincerely, &c."

In a letter to James Madison from Thomas Jefferson, February 15, 1794, Thomas Jefferson wrote about the price of tea —

"Dear Sir

We are here in a state of great quiet, having no public news to agitate us. I have never seen a Philadelphia paper since I left that place, nor learnt any thing of later date except some successes of the French the account of which seemed to have come by our vessel from Havre. It was said yesterday at our court that Genet was to be recalled: however nobody could tell how the information came. We have been told that mr. Smith's speech & your's also on your propositions have got into Davis's papers, but none of them have reached us. I could not have supposed, when at Philadelphia, that so little of what was passing there could be known even

at Kentuckey, as is the case here. Judging from this of the rest of the Union, it is evident to me that the people are not in a condition either to approve or disapprove of their government, nor consequently to influence it. I have been occupied closely with my own affairs, and have therefore never been from home since my arrival here. I hear nothing yet of the second person whom I had engaged as an overseer from the head of Elk, and the first I fear will prove a poor acquisition. Consequently I am likely to lose a year in the reformation of my plantations. The winter has been remarkeably mild — no demand for produce of any kind, at any market of James river. Tobacco & wheat may be bartered at low prices for goods at high. But neither can be sold for cash. This was the state of things at Richmond when business was stopped by the smallpox. Here we can get tea at 2½ Dollars, white sugar at 38 Cents, coffee @ 25. cents &c for wheat @ 66⅔. Accept for yourself, Colo. & mrs. Monroe my affectionate respects
Th: Jefferson"
(Founders, https://founders.archives.gov/documents/Madison/01-15-02-0156

We then move right into the turn of the century with Alexander Hamilton in Scotch Plains, New Jersey, writing to Elizabeth Hamilton on 24 May 1800 requesting more tea —

> "I wrote to you the day before yesterday, my dear Eliza, by Lieutenant Smith. Capt Church informs me he is going to send his servant. I embrace the opportunity of repeating my request for a pair of white Casimer breeches — if not already forwarded by Lt Smith."

"My health continues good and I am under a necessity of playing the game of good spirits — but separated from those I love, it is a most artificial game — and at the bottom of my soul there is a more than usual gloom.

I shall, please God, certainly return at the time prefixed!

God bless you & my beloved Children. Yrs. ever
AH
Send me another half pound of Tea.
Mrs. Hamilton"
(Founders, https://founders.archives.gov/documents/Hamilton/01-24-02-0441)

I think it is safe to say that tea was not only a precious thing to the colonists, but a drink that was both socially, politically, and economically important. Can any other drink claim that status?

CHAPTER 2

Tea Imports to America

Families in the colonies were ordering tea and tea equipment from London throughout the 18th century. Drinking tea became a serious business that included all of the right items in which to partake of it. This chapter focuses on the imports of tea, who purchased them, and when.

Robert Cary & Co., a large London firm deeply involved in the Virginia trade, had long been one of the principal agents for handling the Custis family's business affairs in London, receiving regular consignments of tobacco from Custis plantations and shipping, most recently to Martha Custis, of British goods and supplies that the family required. In 1759, an Account of Goods ordered by Daniel Parke Custis before his death in 1757 is charged to his estate and payment was requested. His widow, Mrs. Martha Dandridge Custis (the future Mrs. George Washington) had received, among other things, of the items imported from

> *Annapolis, October 31, 1771.*
> *Just imported, in the* Brothers, *Captain* Williamson, *from* London, *and will be sold by the Subscribers, at* Mr. Calvert's *old House, on the Publick Circle, near the Market-House in* Annapolis, *wholesale and retail, for ready Money, Bills of Exchange, or short Credit,*
> A Large Assortment and great Variety of European *and* East-India Goods, adapted to the different Seasons: And as ready Money is the best and surest Commodity to go to Market with, such as incline to deal with precious Cash, will, upon Trial, find it much to their Interests in bartering with (tf)
> WALLACE, DAVIDSON and JOHNSON.

Maryland Gazette, Annapolis, October 31, 1771

25

England "Tea of Cartney & Son, and a tea chest and board." The agents were settlings affairs.

In a letter from George Washington to Sarah Cary Fairfax on November 15, 1767, he asks her to spare some Hyson Tea to help him while he is sick. The Hartshorn Shavings were the harts or antlers from young male deer that were used to make gelatin or in his description "Jellys." There were recipes to make Hartshorn Jelly in cookery books of the day.

"Dear Madam

I have lingerd under an Indisposition for more than three Months; and finding no relief above, on the contrary, that I daily grew worse, I have followd (m)y Surgeons advice to leave the place, & try what effects (f)resh Air and Water may have upon my disorder.

On Sunday last I arrivd here, and on Yesterday Mr Green was so kind to favour me with a visit & prescribd to me. He forbids the use of Meats, and substitutes Jelly's and such kind of Food for a constancy: now, as my Sister is from home and I have no Person that has been usd to making these kind of things; and no directions; I find my self under a necessity of applying to you for yr rec[eip]t Book for a little while, and indeed for such materials to make Jellys as you think I may not just at this time have. for I cant get Hartshorn Shavings any where. I must also beg the favour of you to lend me a Pound, or a smaller quantity if you can't spare that, of Hyson Tea. I am quite out & cannot get a supply any where in these parts. please also to lend me a bottle or two of Mountain, or Canary Wine Mr Green directs me to drink a Glass or two of this every day mixd with Water of Gum Arabic.

Pray make my Compliments acceptable to the Young Ladies of Your Family, and believe me to be Dr Madam Yr Most Obedt Servt

Go: Washington"

There are many paintings, diaries, letters and newspaper advertisements that provide some insight into the variety of dry saltery, groceries, and other items imported into the Colonies. We see John Greenhow's store in Williamsburg, Virginia in 1766 offering "chamomile flowers… tea chest furniture and canisters complete…"

Within the Boston Gazette on January 25, 1768, an article submitted by Messeurs Edes and Gill on November 16, 1767 entreated the public that it may be a better idea to grow tea instead of importing it. They suggest that the plant was already being grown in South Carolina and was available in Boston. It was also recommended that old-fashioned herbs as infusions were better than using the traditional tea. At the end of the article, an addendum states, "Since the above came to Hand, we have received information that there is large Quantities of Tea growing at Pepperrellborough Eastward, equal in Quantity to what is imported from the East Indies — the Seed appears exactly the same, and every Fibre of the Leaf agrees; a small Quantity dry'd in a Tea Kettle, and sent to this Town, has been dry'd by good Judges, who tell us that it draws as well, and is as said as good a Flavor as the bohea — large Quantities have been discovered in our South and West Settlements, and as it is a Native of the Country it is doubtful to be found through the Continent. It is thought that when the exact method of curing and drying it is hit upon, we shall not only have a supply for ourselves, but may make a valuable Branch of Export."

From 1771 to 1775, the Annapolis merchant firm of Wallace, Davidson & Johnson imported items entitled "Dry Saltery, Groceries,

Sugar and Lemons" not only for their own store on the city dock in Annapolis, but also for individual customer's special orders as well as other merchants doing business in other parts of the Province. They also imported items for their own stores in Nottingham, Queen Anne, and Pig Point, Maryland.

Order Books dated April 1771 through May 1774 for Wallace Davidson and Johnson, merchants in Annapolis, Maryland included orders from London for Hyson, Congo (good or best Congo), Bohea, or Green tea. They were requested by the one quarter, one half or full chest and/or pound canister full.

On June 4, 1774, several inhabitants of Annapolis as well as in Anne Arundel County agreed to stop the importation of goods from Great Britain not already ordered by July 20. Despite the political leanings of many in Maryland, the orders for these goods from London, to include tea for a future signer of the Declaration of Independence, directed to Joshua Johnson, partner of the firm of Wallace, Davidson & Johnson in London, continued and included good Bohea, best Hyson, and good Congou tea by the chest full. What we do not know is if the order was fulfilled, sent, and/or received.

It is interesting to note that the orders for tea placed by Wallace, Davidson and Johnson for others in the colonies continued after the burning of the ship, the Peggy Stewart, in October 1774. Charles Carroll of Carrollton, a future signer of the Declaration of Independence for Maryland was one of those ordering the importation of tea for his personal use. To explain the Peggy Stewart, it must be noted that in October of 1774, the brigantine Peggy Stewart named after Anthony Stewart's daughter, arrived in the port of Annapolis. Mr. Stewart owned the ship, and it was laden with a cargo of tea. Those contents were subject to being taxed by Britain when it arrived in a port of America. This tax was not accepted by the colonists. In fact, it really made them mad. However, when Anthony Stewart paid the tax to receive his goods, he violated the non-importation resolution imposed by the colonists just five months earlier (May) as mentioned in the *Virginia Gazette*. This payment to receive his goods did not sit well with those living in Annapolis, and when Stewart refused to destroy the tea, the others decided to threaten to burn the ship. Stewart, afraid for his and his family's life, gave in to their demands. He and three others set the ship on fire with the tea within. There is definitely more to this story, but this is essentially a synopsis.

Charles Carroll of Carrolton, as mentioned, continued to order tea with one such request made by Wallace Davidson and Johnson on January 8, 1775 for "12 lbs best congou tea, 1 small chest of bets hyson tea about 70 lbs." It is not known if he received it.

Charles Carroll the Barrister and his wife, Margaret Tilghman Carroll owned porcelain, sepia colored, scenic blue and white, as well as blue and white Worcester China that they probably used for tea. They also owned a copy of *Materia Medica or a Description of Simple Medicines Generally Us'd in Physick,* printed in London in 1716, which mentions the use of tea when used for the sick. This book has a full chapter on tea and mentions the use of it in several receipts for home remedies. I also mention it in Chapter 1.

The order books from Wallace, Davidson, and Johnson in Annapolis, Maryland dated September 29, 1774 had William Bond order tin ware from London that included, "½ doz coffee pots, 1 doz tin nutmeg graters, ½ doz painted sugar boxes, 2 doz 1lb tea canisters, 2 doz ½ lb do, 2 doz pepper boxes, ½ doz tin lanthorns."

Items imported and advertised in the Virginia Gazette included an entry on August 20, 1772 from the ship "Martha" with Captain Brooks from London mentions "tea napkins...Bohea tea, Hyson ditto, Soushong ditto..."

The Margaret Hunter shop in Williamsburg also offered for sale "Hyson and Bohea Teas,"Christopher Hughes, Goldsmith and Jeweler was selling "tea pots, tea spoons, sugar tongs..." among other items as seen in the ads on the following page—

> **Just IMPORTED, and to be SOLD,**
> **By M. HUNTER, in WILLIAMSBURG,**
>
> A GENTEEL Assortment of MILLINERY and other GOODS, consisting of Suits of Blond, Blond Caps, fancied enamelled Stomachers, Italian Ditto, Bath, Brussels, Minionet, and Blond Laces and Edgings, black Laces and Edgings, Silver Blond, Coxcomb Ditto, a Variety of plain and flowered Ribands, white Lustrings, flowered and plain Patent Net, a rich black Patent Net Apron, Patent Net Hoods, Book Muslin Yard and Yard and a Half wide, flowered Ditto, striped and flowered Muslin Yard and Yard and a Half wide, thick Ditto; black, blue, and white Satin for Cloaks; black, blue, and white Persian Ditto; black Mode, white Sarcenet, Suits of Dresden Work, Suits of Childbed Linen, Baskets, Pincushions, Lines, Robes, Cradle Quilts, Paste Necklaces and Earrings, Sprigs and Pins Ditto, Lockets set with Garnets, plain Ditto, Gold and Silver Lockets for Necklaces, Paste and Marcasite Crosses, Foil Stone Ditto, Wax Necklaces and Earrings, Paste and plain Tortoise Shell and Horn Combs, Silver Corals, Paste Buckles, mock and real Garnets; Wax, Coral, and Agate Beads; Ladies Riding Hats, Childrens Beaver Hats, black and blue Satin Caps, quilted Puddings for Children, white and coloured Bone and Ivory Stick Fans, Filagree Toothpick Cases, Silver and Tortoise Shell inlaid with Silver Ditto, white and brown Thread Stockings, ribbed Ditto, Ladies and Gentlemens white Silk Stockings, coloured Ditto, Gresham's Ladies Calimanco Shoes, green and purple Ditto, Ladies black and white Silk Gloves, white and coloured Kid and Lamb Ditto, Mens white Silk Gloves, Wash Leather Ditto; blue, Pink, and white Satin Coats; blue, Pink, white Satin, and Queen's Silk Shoes; Tortoise Shell and Glass Smelling Bottles, Gentlemens and Ladies Pocket Books, Rings, Silver Thimbles, Italian Breast Flowers, small Ditto, Models of Lord Botetourt, Hyson and Bohea Teas, Chip Hats, Cane Ditto, Bonnets, Stuff Petticoats, spotted Gauzes, Apron Ditto, Calicoes and Cottons, Babies of all Prices, a Variety of Toys, green Silk Purses, India Fans, black Pins, Snuff Boxes, Strasburg and Wyfes's Snuffs, Coal Seals, Cottons, Threads, and Tapes.

Virginia Gazette, Purdie & Dixon 14 October 1773

> BALTIMORE, March 27, 1775.
> **CHRISTOPHER HUGHES,**
> **GOLDSMITH AND JEWELLER,**
> At the sign of the Cup and Crown, the south east corner of Market and Gay streets, and opposite Messieurs Usher, Rowe, and company's store, formerly Mr. Little's coffeehouse, in Baltimore town,
>
> BEGS leave to inform his friends, and the public in general, that he hath for sale a neat and elegant ASSORTMENT of PLATE and JEWELLERY, consisting of the following articles, viz. silver coffee pots, tea pots, waiters, tankards, cans, punch strainers, cream ewers, castors, salts and salt glasses, coasters, soup spoons, punch spoons, table and tea spoons, sugar tongs, silver shoe, knee, stock, and breast buckles, plated shoe, knee, and stock buckles, maccaroni shoe buckles, fashionable diamond, topaz, emerald, saphir, amethist, and garnet mens and womens rings, moco paste, foil stone, and plain gold ditto, plain gold and gilt broaches, garnet and paste fancy work ditto, set in gold and silver, garnet, paste, and plain gold mason broaches, and medals, neatly engraved, brown and white chrystal sleeve buttons, set in gold, moco, garnet, and pebble ditto, plain and flowered gold ditto, chrystal, paste, and foyl stone shoe, knee, and stock buckles, plain gold stock buckles, chrystal, mocho, Scotch pebble, paste and glass sleeve buttons in silver, gold, silver, gilt, and pinchbeck seals and trinkets, silver and steel watch chains, tortoiseshell and horn combs, neatly set with paste and marquisets, silver and shagreen watches, watch keys, red Morocco pocket books, with and without instruments, silver spurs, with chains, plated ditto, with and without chains, silver and silver gilt whistle coral and bells, white and red foil, hair lockets, set in gold and fancy work, paste and marquisat necklaces and ear rings, garnet and paste ear rings, draw plates, silver and steel stopped thimbles, pincushion hoops and chains, wax necklace and ear rings, wax and paste pins, hair sprigs, a variety of fashionable stay pins, silver hafted knives and forks in cases, ladies hussifs, with and without instruments, billiard balls, gold scales and weights, properly regulated. Also cutteau du chasse hangers, small swords and pistols of all sorts, true and false stones of all sorts, crucibles, chapes and tongs, binding wire, borax, rotten stone, pumice stone, saltpetre, allum, and a variety of other articles, for the use of silversmiths.
>
> N. B. The highest price will be given for old gold, silver, lace, and watches.

Virginia Gazette, May 18, 1775

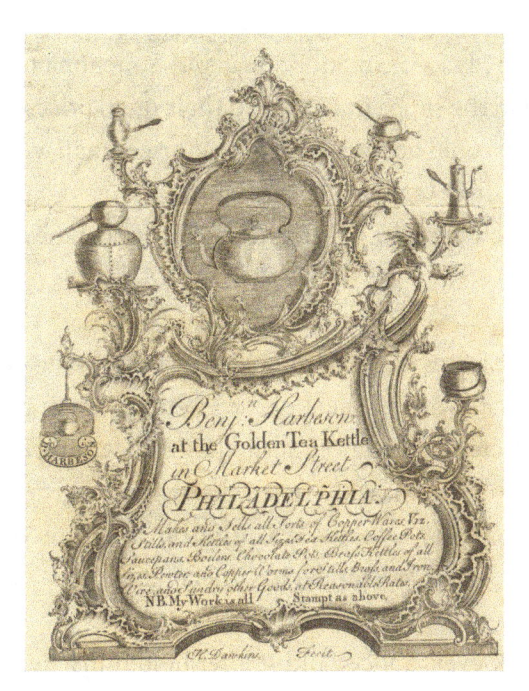

Benjamin Harbeson at the Golden Tea Kettle, 1776, Trade Card, Winterthur

Within the Pennsylvania Gazette dated September 1, 1779, there are extracts from a letter published that mentions a ship captured with her inventory "Sunday last came up to Town the Prize Snow Diana, from London for New York, taken off Sandy Hook by the Holker Privateer, Capt. Geddes. The following is an Inventory of her Cargo, viz. 80 iron cannon, 2, 3, 4 and 6 pounders, with carriages and all other materials compleat; 60 swivels, 10 cohorns 3 pounders, 6 cannonade 12 pounders, and 7m round and bar shot, 155 half barrels powder, 35 boxes, 26 casks, 10 hogsheads, 5 cases, 11 bundles, 1 sheet of lead, 2 bales, 53 coils of cordage and 3 puncheons of naval stores for Goodrich. 32 boxes, 27 chests, 74 casks, 6 hogsheads, 22 cases, 16 trunks, 24 bales, 7 bundles, 6 baskets, 10 firkins, 2 hampers, 4 kegs and 23 packages, about 555 packages in the whole; containing **tea**, loaf sugar, cheese, soldiers clothing, sail cloth, &c. with a great variety of merchandize."

We also see Hyson, Green, Bohea, and Souchona tea being advertised and sold in the shops in 1779, and their retail prices were set by the committees and could not be sold at higher prices than what they set it to.

General Militia Orders printed in the Pennsylvania Gazette for Philadelphia, October 27, 1779 are interesting in that they include rations (last paragraph).

> "THE Classes of the Militia lately called, being designed to co-operate with the fleet of the Count D'Estaing, there will be sufficient time (after authentic advice is received of his arrival on the coast) to reach the rendezvous appointed by his Excellency General Washington. The directions of the President, as Commander in Chief of the Militia, in the mean time, are—
>
> That every officer and soldier hold himself in readiness at a day notice, equipped in the best manner possible, with a due regard to the season. It is expected that tents will be provided for both officers and soldiers, but the insufficiency of the public stores will require their endeavouring to provide themselves with proper clothing. It is expected that every one will bring his own blanket and haversack, and though the march will not probably be long, shoes will be an important article, which it is hoped each militia man will not neglect to procure. Blankets or accoutrements lost, otherwise than by neglect, will be paid for by the public.
>
> Every soldier will bring his arms bright, clean and in good order; his accoutrements compleatly fitted; and the officers are expected to be attentive to this order before they march. The carrying of heavy boxes and trunks has at all times been found so inconvenient, and is so unmilitary, that the President hopes it will not be done on this occasion; and to prevent any

inconvenience to the officers, a number of portmanteaus are provided, for which they will apply (when marching orders are received) to Dr. Jackson, Quarter master of the division, who will deliver them in certain settled proportions.

As the great encouragement given in this service does not seem generally known, the President thinks proper to repeat it on this occasion, viz.

First, One hundred and thirty three dollars and one third of a dollar bounty, of which L 20 in hand when the orders for marching are issued; L 20 to the family, during the absence of the militia man; and the remainder on compleating the term of service.

Second, The usual pay.

Third, Stores to be issued (when in actual service) as to the continental troops, viz. Rum in Spirits at 5s. per gallon; Brown Sugar 3s. 9d. per lb. **Tea** 12s. per ditto; Hard Soap 1s. 3d. per ditto; Tobacco 9d. per ditto.

In 1785, William Jackson advertised at his store on the south west corner of Walnut and Water Streets had for sale, among various goods, "breakfast, green, and bohea teas."

By the end of the century, the new country was figuring out the state and national constitutions as well as laws, taxes, and new duties on imports.

A Sketch of the Proceedings of Congress, House of Representatives of the United States as reported in the Pennsylvania Gazette in April of 1789 says that "The duties on teas were also continued as reported by the committee, except on bohea tea imported from any country other than India or China, or from India or China, in foreign ships; the duty was raised from 8 to 10 cents per pound."

The Pennsylvania Gazette on May 7, 1789 Philadelphia reported that "We hear from New York, that our beloved and illustrious President was proclaimed in a suit of broadcloth manufactured in the state of Connecticut. We hope, from this laudable example in the first and best of men, that we shall soon see industry and oeconomy fashionable in the United States. National dresses and manners, as well as principles, are absolutely necessary to our becoming an independent people."

CHAPTER 3

Social Aspects of Taking Tea

Tea was a social beverage in the early 18th century, and those in America became enamored with drinking it. It was also distinguished as a meal unto itself "to take tea," meant and still means, to have a light meal with the beverage "tea." No other beverage or meal is identified as such to my knowledge.

The serving of it was the greatest mark of civility, and when invited to drink it with the host, it was considered the utmost honor. The ceremony became the very core of family life.

The social aspects of tea were extremely important, especially for the ladies. It was the time of day that allowed them to show off, not only the items they owned that were used for drinking tea, but also the equipment and equipage was important. Those participating would also wear their best clothing, and it was important that their knowledge of the etiquette in serving it to their guests was known. The tea ceremony

Ms. Gonzalez and Ms. McClure in the James Brice House, Historic Annapolis, Maryland

35

was either elaborate in the best and newest taste of the moment or very simple. The most common teas available were Hyson, Soushong, and Bohea although Congo, Gunpowder, and Breakfast are also being advertised. (Roth)

"Taking tea" may also have consisted of a time to discuss the latest news, gossip, play cards or other games, and even dance. Tea was not necessarily done at a specific time of day as it became in later centuries. Bread and butter, cakes, small cakes (cookies), biscuits, creams, cream ices (we know this as ice cream), fruits, sweetmeats (candies, nuts, or candied fruit/nuts), meats, cheeses, fish, etc., were offered as an accompaniment.

Printed in the Pennsylvania Gazette on July 10, 1732, Anthony Afterwit published a letter to "Mr. Gazette." Within the letter, he states that his wife had visited some of her friends who had tea items, and then she, of course, had to have them as well to entertain. He says, " being entertain'd with Tea by the Good Women she visited, we could do no less than the like when they visited us; and so we got a Tea-Table with all its Appurtenances of China and Silver." (Founders, https://founders.archives.gov/documents/Franklin/01-01-02-0080)

Mrs. Afterwit then also published a letter entitled, "The Tea Table" of which the Pennsylvania Gazette reprinted in May 24, 1733 from the Rhode Island Gazette. She writes that she was very happy with tea, but Mr. Afterwit not so much.

> "Tea was as spiricus, and more wholesome than any Strong Drink, be it Punch, be it Wine, be it Cyder, be it Brandy, be it Rum, be it what it will. I confess my covetous Humour and Unacquaintance with Tea had like to have ruin'd me: For the Cups were so small, and the Tea so weak, my Husband said it was like drinking hot water by drops. I therefore bought a large home made Tea-Table, a set of Earthen Plates and Punch Bowls; one of which Bowls (by direction of a Gentle Woman in the Neighborhood) I fill'd with good Strong Tea for my Husband, who then thought it was like drinking. By

Degrees his Desire strong Liquor wholly left him , and he became an Admirer of Tea; but I found the Love of it did not grow upon him so fast as to oblige me to buy larger bowls. In a Months he was contented with the small Tea Table and Cups and Saucers. By his Consent I sold the Punch Bowls to a Tavern Keeper, and (to my Great Comfort) he has not seen them since. His Inclination to Gaming abating, I burnt my Nine-Pins, Frame and all, and dispos'd of all the rest of my Gaming Tools, except the Back-Gammon-Table on which we sometimes take a Game in an Evening or a Cup of Tea in the morning… I am never at a loss for Cream and Butter with my Tea…I am Sir, Yours, &c. Patience Teacraft."

Within the cookery book, "The Whole Duty of a Woman" dated 1737 it mentions that tea was one of those items in "the things to be provided when any Family is going into the Country for a Summer." They included, "Nutmegs, Mace, Cinnamon, Cloves, Pepper, Ginger, Jamaica Pepper, Raisins, Currants, Sugar Lisbon, Sugar Loaf Lump, Sugar double refin'd, Prunes, Oranges, Lemons, Anchovies, Olives, Capers, Mangoes, Oil for Salads, Vinegar, Verjuice, Tea, Coffee, Chocolate, Almonds, Chesnuts, French Pears, Sagoe, Truffles, Morels, Macroni, Vermicelli, Rice, Millet, Comfits, and Pistachoe Nuts."

An unusual story in the Virginia Gazette dated February 28, 1750, mentions a woman who died from "rats poisoning her milk" that she poured in her tea. Her family members that also partook of it also got sick and were not expected to survive.

Within George Washington's diary entry on February 15, 1760, he wrote that tea was offered at the Ball in Alexandria, Virginia.

"Friday Feby. 15th. A Small fine Rain from No. Et. wet the Top of my Hay that had been landed last Night. It was all carted up however to the Barn & the Wet and dry seperated.

Went to a Ball at Alexandria — where Musick and Dancing was the chief Entertainment. However in a convenient Room detachd for the purpose abounded great plenty of Bread and Butter, some Biscuets with Tea, & Coffee which the Drinkers of coud not Distinguish from Hot water sweetned. Be it remembered that pocket handkerchiefs servd the purposes of Table Cloths & Napkins and that no Apologies were made for either. I shall therefore distinguish this Ball by the Stile & title of the Bread & Butter Ball.

The Proprietors of this Ball were Messrs. Carlyle Laurie & Robt. Wilson, but the Doctr. not getting it conducted agreeable to his own taste woud claim no share of the merit of it.

We lodgd at Colo. Carlyles.

A man named Robert Wilson voted for GW in the 1758 Frederick County election for the House of Burgesses.

GW apparently played cards at the ball, because on the following day he recorded the loss of 7s. "By Cards" (Founders, https://founders.archives.gov/documents/Washington/01-01-02-0005-0002)

I came across the most extraordinary article in the The Newbern Gazette dated November 1, 1764, of a woman being shot while having tea with friends (see article on the following page).

The Marquis de Chastellux reminisces in *Voyages de M. le Marquis de Chastellux dans l'Amerique Septentriomale* about his time at Headquarters during the war, "The dinner was excellent, tea followed dinner, and conversation followed tea. All drink tea in America as they drink wine in the south of France. Tea enters into the daily bill of fare. It is on every table but the Colonists banished it with enthusiasm in the early 70's, and dried raspberry leaves were offered to delicate palates — a detestable drink — which they had the heroism to find good."

Social Aspects of Taking Tea

> BOSTON, October 1.
> On Monday last in the Afternoon a very sorrowful Accident happen'd in Cross Street, at the North Part of the Town: Two Lads playing in a Chamber with a Gun, not knowing it to be loaded, presented it out of the Window, to snap it, the Gun went off, and the Shot entered into a neighbouring Window, near which several Women were sitting at a Tea Table; one of them, Mrs. Wheaten, a Widow was shot in the Head in such a Manner that she expired in Three Hours after, another was considerably wounded in the Back part of her head, but not mortally; a third was slightly touch'd each side of her Head by some Shot scattered. It is said this Gun had been loaded with Duck Shot about 5 Months; the Person who used it last returned from Fowling with it loaded; emptied the pan of the priming, and then laid it by, and never was medled with until this shocking Occurence happened.

A Death While Having Tea
The Newbern Gazette, November 1, 1764

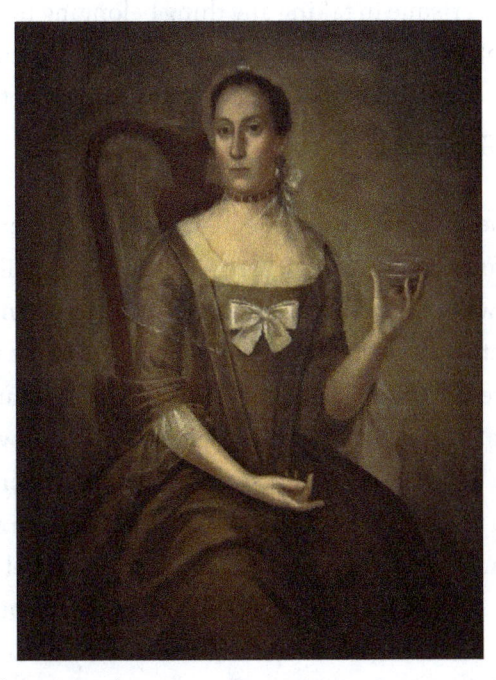

Joseph Badger (1708-1755) American MRS. NATHANIEL LORING (MARY GYLES), c. 1760-63, Oil on canvas, 50 x 39 inches (127 x 99 cm), The Dayton Art Institute, Gift of Sam and Selma Maimon and the Maimon Family, 2002.11

During the war for independence, General George Washington wrote while in camp at Middle Brook on June 6, 1777 that tea was taken as a spoil of war that would be dispersed for the use of the Army and to promote morale—

> "Sir: I this morning received your favour of Yesterday. Inclosed I send you General Orders, which, as far as they apply, are to be strictly attended to. As to the Tea you mention, it is to be sent to the Quarter Master General for the use of the Army; it will be well enough to have the two Teams with their contents sold and the amount divided amongst the Captors, in which number the whole detachment is to be considered, though not immediately with the party. The Spirit and intention of the Orders are, that whenever a party behaves with Bravery and run a risque in taking any thing belonging to the Enemy, the booty so taken, shall be divided amongst them. I am etc. The tea was hidden in "a wood." (GW Papers at the Library of Congress)

Towards the end of the war in September 1783, General Washington wrote to his brother, Bushrod, "There is another thing likewise which I wish to know, without having it known for whom the enquiry is made; and that is, whether French plate is fashionable and much used in genteel houses in France and England; and whether, as we have heard, the quantity in Philadelphia is large, of what pieces it consists, and whether among them, there are Tea urns, Coffee pots, Tea pots, and other equipage for a tea table, with a tea board, Candlesticks and waiters large and small, with the prices of each. These enquiries you may make in behalf of a friend, without bringing my name forward, 'till occasion (if a purchase shou'd happen) may require it." (GW Papers at the Library of Congress)

Letters from America by William Eddis in 1792 mentions that tea was taken just before a couple were to be married. He says, "In this country the marriage ceremony is universally performed in the dwelling houses of the parties. The company, who are invited, assemble early in the evening, and after partaking of tea and other refreshments, the indisputable contract is completed. The bride and bridegroom then receive the accustomed congratulations: cards and dancing immediately succeed: an elegant supper, a cheerful glass, and the convivial song close the entertainment." William Eddis arrived in the colonies in 1769, and was appointed as the Surveyor and Searcher of His Majesties Customs in the Port of Annapolis, Maryland. By 1792, he was back in England having arrived in 1777.

Morning by Richard Houston, 1758, Mezzotint, Yale Center for British Art

Lettered below image is "Ph. Mercier Pinxt. Publish'd according to Act of Parliament Jany. 1758 Rich'd Houston Fecit MORNING. Just risen from Repose fair Delia see, Sipping with secret Joy her favorite Tea; Thus does the Nymph her Morning hours waste, And smiles indulgent on the glad Repast. London, Printed for Robt. Sayer opposite Fetter Lane Fleet Street. Price 1s 6d."

For Breakfast

Tea at breakfast became a popular drink over beer and other spirits. William Byrd II of Virginia wrote in his diary on March 26, 1711, "I rose at 6 o'clock and read nothing. I neglected to say my prayers and ate boiled milk for breakfast and at 9 o'clock I took some milk tea with the company." Milk tea was essentially tea with milk in it.

The naturalist Peter Kalm, during his visit to North America in the mid-18th century, noted that tea was a breakfast beverage in both Pennsylvania and New York. From the predominantly Dutch town of Albany in 1749 he wrote that "their breakfast is tea, commonly without milk. About thirty or forty years ago, tea was unknown to them (before the English settled), and they breakfasted either upon bread and butter, or bread and milk. They never put sugar into the cup, but take a small bit of it into their mouths whilst they drink. Along with the tea they eat bread and butter, with dices of hung beef. Coffee is nor usual here; they breakfast generally about seven. Their dinner is butter-milk, and bread, to which they sometimes add sugar, then it is a delicious dish for them; of fresh milk and bread; or boiled or roasted flesh."

Kalm also wrote that "Tea, coffee, and chocolate, which are at present universally in use here, were then (before the English settled here) wholly unknown. Bread and butter, and other substantial food, was what they break fasted upon; and the above-mentioned superfluities have only been lately introduced, according to the account of the old Swede. Sugar and treacle they had in abundance, as far as he could remember; and rum formerly bore a more moderate price. From the accounts of this old Swede I concluded, that before the English settled here, they followed wholly the customs of Old Sweden; but after the English had been in the country for some time, the Swedes began gradually to follow their customs."

"With the tea was eaten bread and butter or buttered bread toasted over the coals so that the butter penetrated the whole slice of bread. In the afternoon about three o'clock tea was drunk again in the same fashion, except that bread and butter was not served with it." (Roth and Kalm)

Moreau de St. Mery's *American Journey* mentions while on board ship that the American sailor eats four meals a day. "The first being breakfast about seven or eight in the morning; dinner between noon and two, the third is a snack at six, and then supper around eight. Tea is always served at the first meal and constitutes the entire third meal (the snack). They eat salt beef, butter, onions, cheese, and potatoes. He mentions that "they drink a great deal of tea in which sugar is never spared."

Moreau also mentions that in Philadelphia, they breakfast at 9 o'clock on ham or salt fish, herring, and it is accompanied by coffee or tea, slices of tea toasted or untoasted bread spread with butter.

It was described in the Pennsylvania Gazette on April 5, 1753 from Newport, Rhode Island on Wednesday, March 16, at—

> "12 a Clock, a Brigantine from the Bay of Honduras, laden with Longwood, Capt. John Huxham Master, belonging to Mr. Collins, Merchant, of this Place, came ashore on a Sandy Beach about a Mile to the Eastward of the Town, in a violent Gale, the Wind about South, Foresail and Fore-staysail, her Mainsail furl'd, and her Boom lash'd, in the slatboard Crotch. The Weather being very thick, she was first discovered about a Mile from the Shore, and it was supposed that the Hands were all on board, for she shunn'd all Danger, as if steer'd by the skillfulest Pilot, but to the great Surprize of above a

Thousand Spectator, who were immediately on the Beach to give Assistance, they found her entirely abandoned by all the Sailors, there being not one Person on board: By the Order in which their Tea-kettle and other Things appeared in the Cabbin, they had breakfasted, and were preparing for Dinner their Doughboys being made, and a Leg of Pork wash'd ready for the Pot" were found.

The Rev. Andrew Burnaby, A. M., Vicar of Greenwich, was the author of a small publication which appeared in London in 1775, entitled, *Travels Through the Middle Settlements in North America, in the years 1759 and 1760 With Observations upon the State of the Colonies.* His descriptions of the country are quaint and original. In one of his notes he talks about the things eaten at breakfast, which includes drinking tea.

"In several parts of Virginia the ancient custom of eating meat at breakfast still continues. At the top of the table, where the lady of the house presides, there is constantly tea and coffee; but the rest of the table is garnished out with roasted fowls, ham, vension, game and other dainties. Even at Williamsburg, it is the custom to have a plate of cold ham upon the table; and there is scarcely a Virginian lady who breakfasts without it." Mr. Burnaby appears several times in the course of his travels to have visited at Mount Vernon. (Washington Papers)

The print "College Breakfast," while printed in London, shows an interesting look at satire of everyday life. The print is described as "at one end of a long table, a cleric with crossed eyes and mortar board drinks tea. He appears to be suspended in the air (the chair is not drawn) and leans with his elbow on the Morning Herald on the table. At the other end, a yawning academic in an unbuttoned coat under his robe, is doing up his stockings. His loose garter draws the attention of a playful cat while a dog

College Breakfast
J. Nixon invt. et fecit ; Robt. Laurie sculpsit, 1783
Courtesy of the Lewis Walpole Digital Library, Yale University

watches him impatiently. Next to him on the table is an open volume of Euclid's Elements. The maid standing behind the table looks at the cleric on the left and pours hot water on the floor missing the teacup. Above the fireplace hang two muskets and three silhouette portraits of women. The bookshelves on the right display works of English authors and philosophers; on the left hangs a painting of a reposing nude and a satyr."

The Pennsylvania Gazette on July 4, 1792, advertises—

GRAY'S GARDENS.
THE FOURTH OF JULY.

TEA, Coffee, Chocolate, and fruits of the season, will be ready for breakfast. Two tables, one in the Greenhouse and one in the Grove, with 130 covers, furnished with roast beef, rounds, hams, tongues, &c. &c. from morning until night. The number of bars that will be fixed, and plentifully stocked with liquors of the first quality, the wines, &c. kept in reservoirs of water and ice, iced creams of a great variety, fine cakes, &c. to be furnished, and every exertion made to render the entertainment elegant, by the public's.

Very humble Servant,
GEORGE WEED.
Gray's Ferry, July 2d, 1792"

For Supper

Within her book, Colonial Virginia Cookery: Procedures, Equipment, and Ingredients in Colonial Cooking, Jane Carson says that "Tea as a meal between dinner and supper was by no means universal even among ladies of the upper class. When afternoon tea was served, the beverage was accompanied by bread and butter, hot buns or crumpets or muffins, and cake."

Philip Fithian, a tutor at Nomini Hall employed by Colonel Robert Carter in Virginia, wrote in his journal in 1773 that "Mrs. Carter, in the evening, sent me for supper, a Bowl of Hot Green Tea and several tarts…"

He also describes on Sunday, May 29, 1774, "After dinner we had a Grand & agreeable Walk in & through the Gardens — There is great plenty of Strawberries, some Cherries, Goose berries &c. — Drank Coffee at four, they are now too patriotic to use tea." By September of that year, he mentions that "Something in our palace this Evening, very merry happened — Mrs. Carter made a dish of Tea. At Coffee, she sent me a dish & the Colonel both ignorant — He smelt, sipt — look'd — At last with great gravity he asks what's this? — Do you ask Sir — Poh! — And out he throws it splash a sacrifice to Vulcan."

Moreau describes the two o'clock meal while in Philadelphia as going without soup but tea was served at the supper meal. "The dinner consisting of broth, and a main dish of an English roast surrounded by potatoes. Following that are boiled green peas, on which they put butter which the heat melts, or a spicy sauce; then baked or fried eggs, boiled or fried fish, salad which may be thinly sliced cabbage seasoned to each man's taste on his own plate, pastries, sweets to which they are excessively partial and which are insufficiently cooked. For dessert they had a little fruit, some cheese, and a pudding. The entire meal is washed down with cider, weak or strong beer, then white wine. The entrée is accompanied by Bordeaux or Madeira. In the evening at about 7 o'clock, tea is served in the evening as in the morning but without meat when a formal dinner has not been taken. He goes to describe the evening tea ceremony as boring and monotonous! Moreau says that the mistress of the house serves tea, passes it around, and as long as a person has not turned his cup upside down and placed his spoon upon it, just so often will he be brought another cup. Gossip also abounds."

For Guests

> **NEWPORT,** *Dec.* 21.
>
> Last Monday night we had a most violent gale of wind at S. E. S. W. and W. The shipping in the harbour received considerable damage; several small vessels sunk at the wharfs, and some boats were beat to pieces; the brig Sally, Captain Johnson, ready to sail for the West Indies, drove from her anchors, went so high ashore upon Gravelly Point, near the long wharf, as to occasion her being unloaded, in order to get her off; several other vessels were drove from their fasts, as they lay at the wharfs, and were much injured. Quantities of wood, timber, &c. were carried off by the tide, and lost. Almost all the wharfs received very great damage, and some of the principal ones will require large sums of money to put them in repair, occasioned by a very high tide, and the violent agitations of the water.
>
> At an afternoon's visit of a number of Ladies in this town, a few days since, the Lady to whom the visit was paid, being dressed in the manufacture of her own family, the conversation turned upon family industry and economy, and it was resolved that those who could spin ought to be employed that way, and those who could not should reel. When the time arrived for drinking tea, Bohea and Hyperion were provided, and every one of the Ladies most judiciously rejected the poisonous Bohea, and unanimously, to their very great honour, preferred the balsamick Hyperion.

Virginia Gazette, 18 February 1768

When the Marquis de Chastellux was in Philadelphia during his visit from 1779-1785, he describes taking "tea with Madam Shippen" in 1780. He found musical entertainment to meet with his approval and a relationship between the sexes which had parental sanction. One young miss played on the clavichord, and "Miss Shippen sang with timidity but a very pretty voice," accompanied for a time by Monsieur Otto on the harp. Dancing followed, while mothers and other grave personages conversed in another room." (Chastellux)

In a letter from Martha Washington to Abigail Adams on February 20, 1797, she says after Mrs. Adams asked for advice after her husband had won the presidency—

> "It is very flattering for me, my dear Madam, to be asked for rules, by which I have acquired the good opinion, which you say is entertained of me. — With in your self, you possess a guide more certain than any I can give, to direct you: — I mean the good sence and judgment for which you are distinguished; — but more from a willingness to comply with your request, than from any conviction — of the necessity, I will concisely add… The

President having resolved to accept no invitations, it followed of course that I never dined or supped out, except once with the vice President, once with each of the Governers of the state whare we have resided — and (very rarely) at the dancing assemblies. — In a few instances only — I have drank tea with some of the public characters — and with a particular friend or acquaintance." (Founders, https://founders.archives.gov/documents/Adams/04-11-02-0298)

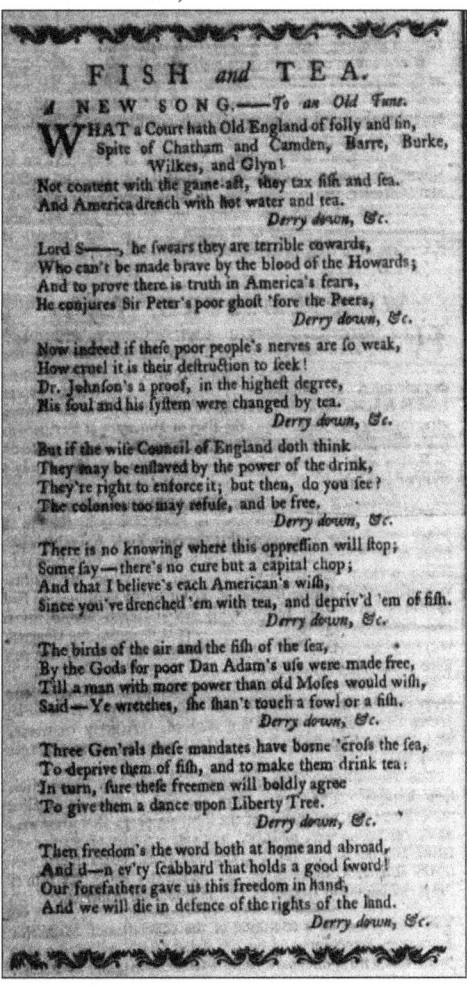

FISH and TEA.

A NEW SONG.—To an Old Tune.

WHAT a Court hath Old England of folly and sin,
Spite of Chatham and Camden, Barre, Burke,
Wilkes, and Glyn!
Not content with the game-act, they tax fish and sea.
And America drench with hot water and tea.
Derry down, &c.

Lord S———, he swears they are terrible cowards,
Who can't be made brave by the blood of the Howards;
And to prove there is truth in America's fears,
He conjures Sir Peter's poor ghost 'fore the Peers,
Derry down, &c.

Now indeed if these poor people's nerves are so weak,
How cruel it is their destruction to seek!
Dr. Johnson's a proof, in the highest degree,
His soul and his system were changed by tea.
Derry down, &c.

But if the wise Council of England doth think
They may be enslaved by the power of the drink,
They're right to enforce it; but then, do you see?
The colonies too may refuse, and be free.
Derry down, &c.

There is no knowing where this oppression will stop;
Some say—there's no cure but a capital chop;
And that I believe's each American's wish,
Since you've drenched 'em with tea, and depriv'd 'em of fish.
Derry down, &c.

The birds of the air and the fish of the sea,
By the Gods for poor Dan Adam's use were made free,
Till a man with more power than old Moses would wish,
Said—Ye wretches, she shan't touch a fowl or a fish.
Derry down, &c.

Three Gen'rals these mandates have borne 'cross the sea,
To deprive them of fish, and to make them drink tea:
In turn, sure these freemen will boldly agree
To give them a dance upon Liberty Tree.
Derry down, &c.

Then freedom's the word both at home and abroad,
And d—n ev'ry scabbard that holds a good sword!
Our forefathers gave us this freedom in hand,
And we will die in defence of the rights of the land.
Derry down, &c.

Virginia Gazette, July 15, 1775

Coffee Houses, Taverns, Public Houses, Inns, and Entertainment

> **Samuel Richardet,**
>
> Respectfully informs the Gentlemen, Merchants, &c. that he has this day opened the
> **CITY TAVERN AND MERCHANT's COFFEE-HOUSE,**
> In the City of Philadelphia.
>
> The Subscription Room will be furnished with all the daily papers published in Philadelphia, New-York, Boston, Baltimore, &c. together with those of the principal commercial cities of Europe. They will be regularly filed and none permitted to be taken away on any account.
>
> Tea, Coffee, Soups, Jellies, Ice Creams, and a variety of French liquors, together with the usual refreshments, will at all times be procured at the bar.
>
> Gentlemen may depend on being accommodated with the choicest Wines, Spiritous Liquors, and the most approved Malt Liquors, from the London and other breweries.
>
> The Larder will be supplied with the prime and earliest productions of the season. Large and small parties, or single gentlemen, may be accommodated with Breakfast, Dinner, or Supper at hours most convenient to themselves. A cold collation is regularly kept for gentlemen's conveniency.
>
> The bill of fare to be had at the bar.

The Pennsylvania Gazette, May 20, 1796

The colonists established their coffee houses after those in England. At one point, they were proud to be Englishmen and probably conducted themselves the same way as well with some slight variations. These establishments consisted of mostly male clientele. Besides coffee, they also served chocolate and tea, or maybe offered a pipe. They could talk about the latest news and gossip, Lawyers would discuss the law or literature; or, possibly criticize the latest play. There were coffee houses for men of all classes, and each had their favorite. (Roth & Timbs)

Taverns in the colonies operated under a license just as they did in England. Each colony had different ways in which to apply, and the timeframe in which they were approved and remained in affect also varied.

"By the Council in Assembly April 8th 1706,

"read and referred till the Afternoon Brought into the House the Petition of Mary Newell which was read and ordered to be entered Viz., To his Excy the Govr her Maj'ty's Honble Council & the Genl Assembly. The humble Petition of Mary Newell of Annapolis, humbly sheweth, that your Petitioner hath been a very laborious and Painstaking woman for several years in this Province and hitherto hath maintained herself by her Drudgery. But now may it please your Excy & Honours She finds old Age and Impotency has much impeded her that she cannot longer scuffle in the world so to provide herself with Necessaries as formerly she was able to do Therefore humbly addresses herself to your Excy & Honours humbly requesting Leave to vend Coffee Tea and a Dram Not that She is in the least desirous to keep a Tipling House or any Thing tending to Excess and Intemperance but purely to capacitate herself to get an honest Livelyhood without being burthensome to any Body I humbly implore your Excy and Honours out of your Abundance of your Consideration and Pity will be pleased to grant Relief in the Premises And as in duty bound will ever pray. The above Petition was by the Council indorsed thus." (Maryland State Archives)

Within the *Secret Diary of William Byrd II of Virginia, 1709-12*, on October 29, 1710 he writes, "I rose at 6 o'clock and sent away my man Tom home with a letter to my wife. I read two chapters in Hebrew and some Greek in Homer. I said my prayers and ate boiled milk for breakfast. I went to church about 11 o'clock and heard a sermon of Mr. Taylor. Then Colonel Duke and I went to Mr. Commissary's to dinner and Mr. Hamilton the general postmaster with us. I ate roast mutton. I had a great deal of wit this day, more than ordinary. My cousin Harrison and her daughter were here. About 5 o'clock we took our leave and walked to the coffeehouse where I drank two dishes of tea. Here I sat till 8 o'clock and then returned to my chambers where I read some verses of the Commissary's making. I said my prayers and had good health, good thoughts, and good humor, thank God Almighty. I committed uncleanness this night, for which God forgive me.

In a letter from Benjamin Franklin to his sister, Jane, on January 6, 1727, he writes —

Dear Sister,

I am highly pleased with the account captain Freeman gives me of you. I always judged by your behaviour when a child that you would make a good, agreeable woman, and you know you were ever my peculiar favourite. I have been thinking what would be a suitable present for me to make, and for you to receive, as I hear you are grown a celebrated beauty. I had almost determined on a tea table, but when I considered that the character of a good housewife was far preferable to that of being only a pretty gentlewoman, I concluded to send you a spinning wheel, which I hope you will accept as a small token of my sincere love and affection.

Sister, farewell, and remember that modesty, as it makes the most homely virgin amiable and charming, so the want of it infallibly renders the most perfect beauty disagreeable and odious. But when that brightest of female virtues shines among other perfections of body and mind in the same person, it makes the woman more lovely than an angel. Excuse this freedom, and use the same with me. I am, dear Jenny, your loving brother,

B. Franklin
(Founders, https://founders.archives.gov/documents/Franklin/01-01-02-0031)

Social Aspects of Taking Tea

George Washington wrote in his diary, in 1760, on Friday, February 15 that tea was offered at a ball in Alexandria — "A Small fine Rain from No. Et. wet the Top of my Hay that had been landed last Night. It was all carted up however to the Barn & the Wet and dry seperated. Went to a Ball at Alexandria — where Musick and Dancing was the chief Entertainment. However in a convenient Room detachd for the purpose abounded great plenty of Bread and Butter, some Biscuets with Tea, & Coffee which the Drinkers of coud not Distinguish from Hot water sweetned. Be it remembered that pocket handkerchiefs servd the purposes of Table Cloths & Napkins and that no Apologies were made for either. I shall therefore distinguish this Ball by the Stile & title of the Bread & Butter Ball. The Proprietors of this Ball were Messrs. Carlyle Laurie & Robt. Wilson, but the Doctr. not getting it conducted agreeable to his own taste woud claim no share of the merit of it. We lodgd at Colo. Carlyles." The following day he recorded that "the loss of 7s. By Cards." (GW Papers at the Library of Congress)

On May 15, 1766, The Pennsylvania Gazette shows William Johnson opening a "House of Entertainment" and offering "To the PUBLICK. THE SUBSCRIBER having opened a House of Entertainment for Coffee, Tea, and Cheesecakes, in the Town of Bath, opposite the Bath House, having commodious Rooms therein, and as it is in a pleasant Situation, hopes it will suit those that are inclinable to retire for the Benefit of their Health, where they shall meet with good Attendance…"

In the Pennsylvania Gazette on June 23, 1773, Thomas Mushett advertises 21 June that "…having taken that large and commodious TAVERN, at the sign of the BUCK, on the five mile round, lately occupied by Mr. DANIEL GRANT, begs leave to inform the public, that he has furnished the said house in a neat and genteel manner for the accommodation of company. Those who please to favour him with their custom, may be assured of his best endeavours to merit their approbation. Bespoke dinners or entertainments will be carefully attended to. Ladies and gentlemen that ride for the benefit of the air, may have **tea** and coffee, morning and evening.

On March 9, 1775, within the Virginia Gazette, Mr. William Dawson wrote to Mr. Pinkney, the following, "I THINK the following patriotic and candid behaviour of Mrs. NEW, of Gloucester county, deserves a place in year paper. I am Sir, your humble servant."

> "Not long ago, some gentlemen travellers went to Mr. New's (who was then landlord of an inn) and tarried the night. In the morning they desired Mrs. New to get TEA for breakfast: She at first told them that it was not agreeable to the resolutions entered into by the provincial congress to use it; but they still insisting that they would have it, if there was any in the house sine therefore brought all five had to breakfast, and afterwards, in the presence of the, gentleman, committed every ounce she had left to the flames, adding these words, "If I had said that I had not any tea in the house I should have told you an untruth; but now I do, with truth, that I have none; not will I use any until the unhappy different between Great Britain and her colonies shall subside."

MATTHEW MOODY advertised in the Virginia Gazette on April 28, 1775, that "Jun living at the lowest House at the Capitol Landing, begs Leave to acquaint the Publick that he keeps, at all Times, fine Queen's Creek OYSTERS, fresh from the Rock, which will be dressed agreeable to the Taste of those who may please to favour him with their Custom, and with the greatest Expedition. — TEA and COFFEE to be had likewise, if required; and a good BOWL of PUNCH."

At a large gathering, a tray was often employed for passing refreshments and "a servant brings in on a silver tray the cups, the sugar bowl, the cream jugs, pats of butter, and smoked meat, which are offered to each individual." (Roth)

Social Aspects of Taking Tea

> **St. Tammany's Wigwam.**
>
> THE subscriber having rented that pleasant situation, the Seat of Mr. Edward Pole, on Race street and the Banks of Schuylkill, between the Upper and Middle ferries, begs leave to inform the Public in general, and his Friends in particular, that he has Opened a Genteel House of Entertainment; for which purpose he has supplied himself with a stock of the best Liquors—Where any Parties, either Gentlemen or Ladies, may be furnished with the best Entertainment at any time: also, Tea, Coffee, and Chocolate at any hour. And as——
>
> **BATH HOUSES**
>
> Are now erecting on the premises, viz. a Hot Bath, Cold Bath, and Shower Bath, which will be ready by the spring, together with a number of new Summer Houses; and from the pleasantness of the situation, and the prospect of the beautiful river Schuylkill, he flatters himself it is as well adapted for a Genteel House of Entertainment as any one near the City. Any Gentleman wishing to amuse themselves, either in
>
> **The Fowling or Fishing**
>
> Way, may be furnished with Boats and Fishing Tackle, and Fowling Pieces, together with Powder and Shot, at any time.
> There is on the Premises, an Excellent
>
> **Mineral Spring.**
>
> Every Pains will be used by the Subscriber; and his whole time devoted to render satisfaction to such Gentlemen and Ladies as please to honor him with their Company.   GEORGE SAVELL.
> November 4.   f.w.f.

Philadelphia Gazette, November 17, 1765

Hospitals and Medicinal Uses

William Byrd wrote in his diary on February 5, 1711, "I rose about 8 o'clock and found my cold still worse. I said my prayers and ate milk and potatoes for breakfast. My wife and I quarreled about her pulling her brows. She threatened she would not go to Williamsburg if she might not pull them; I refused, however, and got the better of her, and maintained my authority. About 10 o'clock we went over the river and got to Colonel Duke's about 11. There I ate some toast and canary. Then we proceeded to Queen's Creek, where we found all well, thank God. We ate roast goose for supper. The women prepared to go to the Governor's the next day and my brother and I talked of old stories. My cold grew exceedingly bad so that I thought I should be sick. My sister gave me some sage tea and leaves of [s-m-n-k] which made me mad all night so that I could not sleep but was much disordered by it. I neglected to say my prayers in form but had good thoughts, good humor, and indifferent health, thank God Almighty."

Within the Pennsylvania Packet on May 11, 1772, a letter was published from the dead to the living, "you will oblige one of your female readers" where she claims to have died from drinking tea—

> TO Miss Charlotte in Westmorland, "My Dear Friend, The friendship which I professed to you while living, continues even after my death — an event, of which, I dare say, my friends, particularly my brother, has informed you. As my correspondence with you was interrupted by the peculiar nature of my disorder for several years, before it put an end to my life, I shall beg leave to give you a detail of the manner in which it attacked me; but shall first mention the cause of it, and then inform you of the steps by which it advanced, till it lodged me at last in the silent mansions of the dead. — You may remember, that I carried with me to Philadelphia, a constitution which was naturally fine, and which had been proof against all the multitudes of the cold and moisture of my native climate. — I had been early taught to avoid singularity in my dress, behavior, and diet, and that a decent conformity of the customs of the different companies or countries we went into, was the truest mark of a polite education. This led me to fall in with the general custom which prevails in the country of *drinking* tea, as it is called. The herb of which it is made grows in China, and in several parts of the East Indies. It is a shrub, the leaves of it are only used in tea. They are either

Social Aspects of Taking Tea

plucked, or drop naturally from the shrub, and from these two circumstances, they are altered considerably in their quantities, so as to acquire the name of *Green* in the former, and of Bohea in the latter case. After this they are dried upon a plate of copper. They are of a very astringent nature, and so very nauseous, that even those who have lived longest upon the tea, cannot drink it, without mixing large quantities of sugar and cream with it, which in some measure destroys its disagreeable taste. — A tea made of these leaves is used twice a day. — In the morning, by way of breakfast and in the afternoon, by way of refreshment. — It is drank almost boiling hot, at all seasons, even in the heat of summer. The women are such slaves to it, that they would rather go with-out their dinners than without a dish of tea, as they call it in the afternoon. Although it was extremely disagreeable to me at first, yet the same practice which makes snuff, tobacco, and spirituous liquors agreeable, (from each of which nature shudders the first time we take them) in a few months rendered even this tea agreeable to me. I had not long taken a pleasure in drinking it, before I was afflicted with a violent pain in my stomach and bowels. This was attributed to cold, and to some bad quality in the water in which the tea was infused, and medicines were administered for my relief. Soon after this, I was afflicted with a trembling in my limbs, which, as it was increased after every time I drank tea, led me to suspect that this was the cause of it; and I should have dropped it immediately, had not an old woman of eighty assured me, that she had drank is constantly for fourty-seven years, without feeling the least convenience from it. The symptoms of my disorder increased daily. Upon asking of my physician what he thought of my using tea in my diet; he told me, that it was a harmless thing, and that the ill consequences that it sometimes produced, depended on the warm water we drank with it, which was always hurtful as the proportion as the tea was weak; he advised me, therefore, to drink my tea stronger for the future, and to never let it be above milk warm. With this piece of advice, he gave me a quantity of what they call foetid medicines, which I afterwards found were composed of the excrementitious substances of animals and vegetables, the taking of which was a greater punishment to me than the complicated evils I had experienced before, especially as I found not the least benefit from them. On the contrary, my disorder grew worse, attended with a number of new sumptoms.... From a want of appetite, was obliged to leave off drinking tea, and from the temporary relief which this, together with the mineral water gave me, I was convinced, had I dropped the one and been sent to the other a little sooner, I should have recovered from my disorder. But Heaven had ordered it otherwise... Your affectionate Julia.

In Camp near York, November 3, 1781, an entry was made by William Stephens Smith for "Articles wanted for the use of the General Hospital at Williamsburgh.

- 800 Weight of brown Sugar
- 1 Hhd. of Molasses
- 120 lbs. Bohea Tea
- 2 Hhds. of Rum
- 2 Quarter Casks of Port or Maderia *Wine*"
(GW Papers at the Library of Congress)

"*Sage* by Virtue of its volatile and aromatick Salt expels the Courses of Women, comforts the Brain, and cleanses the Womb: They commonly make a sort of Tea of Sage leaves. (Pitton de Tournefort)

"The infusion of leaves of *Betony* made after the manner of Tea, is good in Distempers of the Stomach and Head."

NOTE: Betony in Latin is "Stachys Officinalis," commonly known as common hedge nettle, betony, purple betony, wood betony, bishop wort, or bishop's wort and a member of the mint family. (Pitton de Tournefort)

"The leaves of *Water Germander* are sometimes taken in the manner of Tea, to restore a dejected Appetite, and to give Ease in the gouty Pains…" (Pitton de Tournefort)

NOTE: Water Germander is scarcely used now as a medicine.

The Pennsylvania Gazette advertises the following for Medicinal waters on May 12, 1790, "For Drinking and Bathing, at HARROWGATE, within four miles of the city of Philadelphia, near the Frankford road" and includes tea—

> "THE Author of Nature having provided the above named spot with three different kinds of mineral waters, the subscriber has, at a considerable expence, erected such buildings over them, as will render them fit to be used either internally or externally, according to the diseases of the persons who required them."
>
> "These waters have been repeatedly examined by Doctors Rush and Moyes."
>
> "The first spring contains a quantity of sulphurous, or what those gentlemen call hepatic air, and a small quantity of iron; it is remarkably light, and resembles, both in composition and medicinal qualities, the famous Harrowgate waters in England."
>
> "The second spring contains a quantity of fixed air with a small quantity of iron and calcareus earth, and possesses many of the virtues of the Pyrmont waters, so well known, and as justly celebrated all over the world."

"The third spring is a common chalybeate water, and resembles the Bristol, of this state.

The subscriber submits it to the judgment of the physicians of Philadelphia, when, in what diseases, and in what quantity, to recommend the use of these waters: he will only observe, that the Harrowgate waters have rendered essential service to persons afflicted with diseases and obstructions of the stomach, bowels and kidnies: they have also removed worms, and relieved the irregular gout and chronic rheumatism; externally applied, these waters have, in many instances, cured ulcers and other eruptions of the skin."

"In the house erected over Harrowgate waters, are two shower baths and two dressing rooms, and at the chalybeate spring is a convenient bath for plunging or swimming."

"For the use of these baths the price will be four dollars the season, two dollars for one month, five shillings for one week, one shilling for each time the baths are used less than a week, and two dollars the season to those who drink the waters only; and the Public may rest assured, that neither expence nor troubles shall be spared to render these baths and waters useful and convenient."

"Breakfasts, dinners, suppers and lodging, in the genteelest manner and on the shortest notice, may be had at Harrowgate Inn, adjoining the springs; and if four or more ladies or gentlemen will subscribe for the use of the Harrowgate light-waggon in the mornings, it shall run every day, and set out from Mr. Hay's Inn, in Race street, precisely at 6 o'clock."

"THE subscriber also respectfully informs his Friends in particular, and the Public in general, that a CONCERT of VOCAL and INSTRUMENTAL MUSIC, with ILLUMINATION, in imitation of the European Vauxhall, will commence on Thursday the 13th instant, at Harrowgate, at 4 o'clock, P.M. The Illumination to begin at 7, and the whole conclude precisely at 9 o'clock in the evening; and, if encouragement is given will be continued on every succeeding Thursday during the season, weather permitting."

"The rural situation, and many natural beauties of Harrowgate, are so well known, that a particular description of them is unnecessary; it is decorated with summer-houses, arbors, walks, seats, &c. The new house is spacious, and contains a saloon for balls, and a number of other rooms for companies or parties, large and small."

"A good and plentiful table, with liquors of the best quality, teas, coffee, fruit in season, will be furnished on the shortest notice, and every attention paid to render the entertainment commodious, elegant and agreeable."

"Any communication for improvements will be gratefully received and attended to, by the Public's most obedient and most humble servant,"

"G. ESTERLY."

"Harrowgate, May 3, 1790.

N.B. The Harrowgate light waggon will also run in the afternoon of every day after the 13th instant, and set out from Mr. Hay's Inn, precisely at 3 o'clock, and return in the evening, at the moderate rate of 2 s. each person."

"The Dutch merchant Andreas Everardus van Braam Houckgeest, who became a naturalized American citizen in 1784, arrived in Philadelphia onboard the ship, *Lady Louisa*, from the imperial court of China with "A Box of China for Lady Washington" on 24 April 1796."

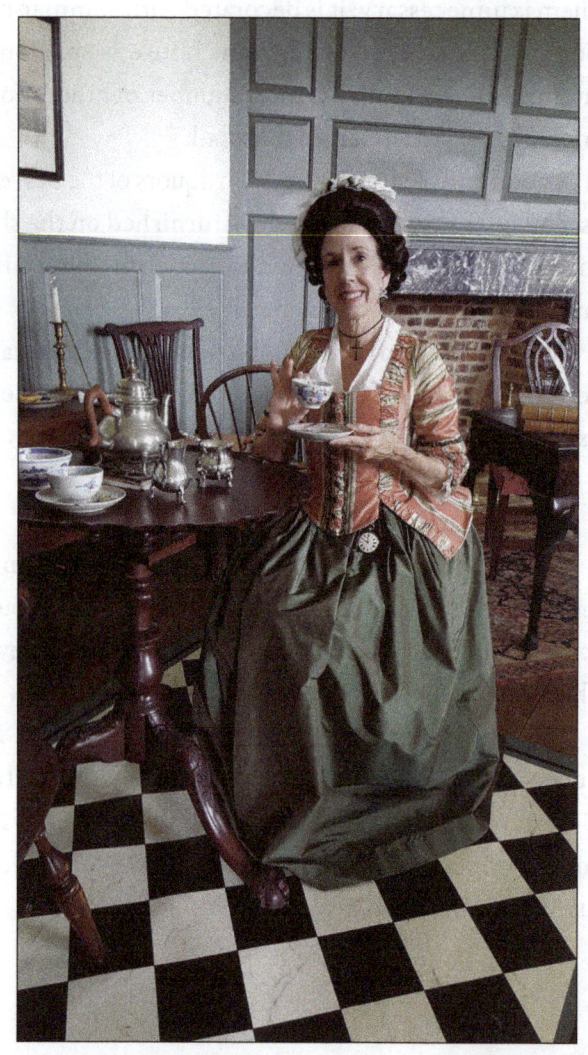

Ms. McClure taking tea in Patrick Henry's Home in Scotchtown, Virginia

CHAPTER 4

The Tea Ceremony

The Marquis de Barbe-Marbois remarked in his diary, American Journey, that those taking tea "seat themselves at a spotless mahogany table, and the eldest daughter of the household or one of the youngest married women makes the tea and gives a cup to each person in the company. During the tea hour, social and economic affairs were discussed and when there is no news at all, they repeat old stories."

I decided to check the John Ash Dictionary of 1775 to see if there were definitions of tea and items related to drinking it. The sources that I have come across do not identify the same items used during tea. The social economic status of a person or family is key in that. Not everyone could afford all of the items that were supposedly needed to take it as was proper per social norms of the time. However, that did not stop those from trying! John Ash did not disappoint me. In his dictionary are defined several types of tea and tea related items—

> **Bohea** — A species of tea, tea of the darker colour and most commonly drank.
> **Congou** — A kind of tea, fine bohea.
> **Hyson** — A kind of fine tea. Belonging to a fine kind of tea.
> **Pekol** — A kind of tea.

Souchong — A kind of fine bohea tea.

Tea — A Chinese plant, the dried leaves of the plant, an infusion of the dried leaves of the plant now commonly drank in most parts of Europe. Belonging to tea, used with tea.

Tea Board — The moveable board or plain surface on which the teacups are placed.

Tea Canister — A canister to keep tea in.

Tea Chest — A small kind of cabinet in which tea is brought to table.

Tea Cup — The small cup in which tea is usually drank.

Tea Dish — A tea cup, usually without handles.

Tea Kettle — The vessel in which water is boiled for tea.

Tea Leaf — The leaf of the tea tree.

Tea Leaves — The leaves of tea.

Tea Pot — The pot or vessel in which tea is made.

Tea Spoon — The spoon used in drinking tea.

Teacupful — As much as can be contained in a teacup.

Teaspoonful — As much as can be contained in a teaspoon.

Roth describes the tea ceremony starts with the lady of the house, seated at the tea table, measuring out dry tea leaves from the canister into its lid. Others at tea, family and guests, stand or sit nearby and observe. A servant stands ready with hot water from the kettle to pour the boiling water over the leaves once they are in the teapot. The kettle is either placed on a nearby stand or taken back to the fire to remain hot to either rinse the cups or dilute the tea.

She then goes into mentioning that the way the hostess knows you do not want any more tea to be served, you must turn your cup over and place your spoon on top. This is the signal. Several things can be served at tea: cakes, cold pastries, sweetmeats, preserved fruits, plates of cracked nuts, apples, smoked meats, etc. A teatime was also enjoyed by having a musical entertainment, dancing, or playing cards and games, or social and economic affairs discussed, gossip is exchanged.

Jeremy describes in *Henry Wansey and His American Journal 1794* that Mrs. Washington was known to make the tea and coffee for guests and "on the table were two small plates of sliced tongue, dry toast, bread and butter, etc., but no broiled fish, as is the general custom. There was little appearance of form: one servant only attended, who had no livery; a silver urn for hot water, was the only article of expense on the table." The "tongue" was probably beef.

In the time period, a dish of tea was in reality a cup of tea, for the word "dish" meant a cup or vessel used for drinking as well as a utensil to hold food at meals. John Ash, as we have noted, defined a Tea Dish as a tea cup. A play on this word is evident in the following exchange reported by Philip Fithian between himself and Mrs. Carter, the mistress of Nomini Hall, one October forenoon in 1773: "Shall I help you, Mr. Fithian, to a Dish of Coffee? — I choose a deep Plate, if you please Ma'am, & Milk." This suggests that the practice of saucer sipping, while it may have been common among the general public, was frowned upon by polite society. Americans preferred and were "accustomed to eat everything hot" further explains why tea generally was drunk from the cup instead of the saucer. According to Peter Kalm, "when the English women [that is of English descent] drank tea, they never poured it out of the cup into the saucer to cool it, but drank it as hot as it came from the teapot." Roth mentions that on the table a saucer seems to have always been placed under the cup, whether it was right side up, or right side down.

Roth also mentions that teaspoons in use may have been placed on the saucer or in the cup. Tongs were suited for lifting the lumps of sugar from the container into the teacup. Arched and scissor types were used. They had flat grips for holding a lump of sugar. It seems that they were named tongs, tea tongs, spring tea tongs, and sugar tongs, normally made of silver but ivory and wooden tea tongs were advertised in the Pennsylvania Journal in 1763 for sale.

She then further goes into describing sugar dishes or sugars came in various materials that often matched the tea set. They were available in delftware, blue and white burnt, enameled, and penciled china. They came with covers, but sugar boxes, basins, plated sugar baskets were also used as containers. The covers or lids of the sugar dishes were suggested that the saucer shape cover of the hemispherical sugar dish or bowl, fashionable in the first half of the 18th century, also served as a spoon tray or for use under the tea pot to protect the table. Containers for cream and milk seen made of glass, pewter, silver, pensiled or burnt china, or even enameled.

The following description of how to make a good cup of tea is long but essential for you to read, at least once. It is taken from the *Domestic Management, or the Art of Conducting a Family; with Instructions to Servants in General Addressed to Young Housekeepers.*

> **"ART of making good TEA, with a small Quantity of the Herb.**
>
> AS it frequently falls to upper maids and footmen, to make Tea apart, for company, and few know how to make it well, a little instruction on this head, it; is hoped, will not offend them. Indeed, there are few young house-keepers, but need some information on this subject.
>
> I must compare making of Tea to brewing. There are few country servants, but under take to brew, and no one in 20 makes good beer; so one and all, know how to make Tea, and yet few make it good. As the chief art in brewing is to make strong beer with as little result as possible, so, in making Tea, the chief art, is to make it strong, without waste. The method then; as it follows:
>
> The tea-pot should be of a size, proportioned to the number of persons that are to be served, and the size of the cups. If six persons are to drink Tea, the pot should hold as much as will fill nine cups; and one tea-spoonful is sufficient for each person to have three cups of tea, which is the general quantity drank by each. Six tea-spoonful is about half an ounce; three being

13 in one ounce. These should be put into the pot, and boiling water poured on, until the pot is one-third full. It should thus stand a quarter of an hour, which will draw a good tincture.

In the mean time, boiling water should be poured into the cups, to heat them; for, unless Tea is served hot; it is little better than slop. When the Tea is sufficient drawn; the tea-cups should be emptied; the pot filled up with boiling water (not water that has boiled, but boiling) and each cup should instantly be filled. The tincture of Tea in the pot will make the whole sufficiently strong; and the boiling water added, will make the whole sufficiently hot.

After filling the six cups, the pot will remain one-third full; as before; and will draw the Tea, and add strength to it. When the cups are returned, if the kettle is at hand, (as it always should be), the cups should be washed with clean boiling water, not washed in the bason, into which the slop has been thrown.

After this, fill up the pot a second time, and pour it off immediately, and the second round of cups will be equally strong and hot, as the first. The Tea then in the pot left, will be also one-third of its contents, which is so to continue, till the cups are to be filled a third time, the pot will be quite empty, and the strength of the Tea all served; whereas many, by pouring too much water on the leaves at last, will make the last round of Tea weak, and leave two or three cups of good Tea in the pot, to be thrown away.

By this mode of making Tea, it will be all uniformly strong, and all served up hot. Should any of the company want a fourth, or fifth Cup, another tea-spoonful of Tea should be added to the pot, a little boiling water poured over it, and time allowed it to draw, or extract its strength, and the whole should be managed as before. It is the best way, and most agreeable to everyone, to send round the sugar and cream with the cup, and let each person take what he pleases.

If tea is made in the adjoining room, and sent in, the best method is to put a tea-spoonful of tea for each person, into a pot that will contain as many cups as there are persons, and fill it up, letting it stand a quarter of an hour; or longer, and when it is to be served, pour as much tea from the pot as will fill each cup one third full, and fill it up from a kettle with boiling water. This will make the tea equally good, as if managed in the other way.

If a chamber-maid is employed to spread bread and butter for tea, it is not necessary that the mark of her thumb should be imprinted on every slice; nor that she, on quitting the loaf, leave all the holes full of butter."

CHAPTER 5

Tea Equipage

It was important to have the correct tea items. I, again, go to Rodris Roth's book as she describes that a well-equipped tea table would contain a teapot, plate for the teapot, slop bowl, container for milk

The Tea Table, photo taken at Patrick Henry's Home in Scotchtown, Virginia. In this photo are clockwise — slop bowl, tea caddy, tea cup with saucer and spoon, sugar bowl with scissor tongs, mote spoon, creamer, tea cup with saucer and spoon, and the tea pot is in the middle with a ceramic tile underneath to protect the table

69

or cream, a tea canister, sugar container, tongs, teaspoons, cups, and saucers. The cups and saucers should all match and be of the same set. These are a necessity for an appropriate tea ceremony. All tea items should be prominently displayed on the tea table, and not stored in the cupboards or closets. It is of the best fashion to use a circular table on a pillar with three legs of walnut or mahogany. (NOTE: This was probably a tilt top table where the top unlatched underneath to fold vertically.) The tea table is kept against a wall until required. A cloth need not be used, but truth be told is all dependent if one is available. However, a tray or teaboard can also be used at breakfast or morning tea or when there is nothing else available. A caddy or canister of tea should also be nearby or on the table.

Even during the war and while encamped, General Washington wrote to Captain Gibbs while at White Plains, on August 4, 1778 the following—

> "Dear Gibbs: — If your attempt upon Rhode Island should prove [fortunate], and I think there is scarce a possibility of its failure, unless a superior Fleet should compel Count d'Estaing to quit his station; you will have it much in your power to provide for the use of this family, many articles of which you know we stand in much need — as also some things which I should be glad to procure for my own use — among which I find myself in want of a genteel cutting sword. — I do not mean a true horseman's sword; and yet one fit for riding. Many things among the officer's baggage, if it should happen to fall into the hands of our troops, or should be sold by themselves, might be convenient for me; such as table and other camp equipage, properly assorted and contrived for stowage. To be particular in the recital of my wants I cannot, not having time for recollection. — Your knowledge of them, reminded by what you may see, will prove more adequate than vague directions. **Tea equippage, plates and dishes, bowls, basins, camp stools, are essentially necessary; — such of them as**

Tea Equipage

can be procured, of materials not liable to break, should be preferred. The money necessary for the purchase of these things will be advanced by General Greene, upon showing him this letter. I most sincerely wish success to the enterprize, and much honor and reputation to yourself, being with great truth and sincerity Your affectionate, Geo. Washington. (GW Papers at the Library of Congress)

> To be SOLD, on Monday the 4th of August, at mr. Montgomerie's storehouse in the town of Dumfries, either for ready money, or twelve months credit upon bond and good security,
>
> SUNDRY valuable household goods, consisting of beds, bedsteads and curtains, counterpanes, blankets, table and bed linen, tables, chairs, tea and table china, china bowls, queen's china, drinking glasses and tumblers, a variety of other articles, a considerable quantity of kitchen furniture, and a fashionable phaeton.
>
> July 15. 1777.

Virginia Gazette, July 25, 1777

"Tea ceremony" equipage can consist of —

- Tea Board that sits on the Tea Table
- Tea Tray
- Tea Kettle
- Water Urn
- Tea Canister
- Teapot
- Tea Cups
- Saucers
- Slop Bowl
- Milk or Cream Container
- Sugar Container
- Tongs
- Tea spoons
- Strainer
- Mote Spoon
- Tea Napkins
- Tea Table

The Tea Table, Jno. Bowles Print, 1710
Courtesy of the Lewis Walpole Collection, Yale University

"A group of ladies sit in highback chairs around a circular table, drinking tea and gossiping. On the table in front of the lady on the right, lays a book open to pages which read "Chit-Chat"; her lap dog sits looking up at her eagerly while a demon hides under the table at her feet. The ladies sit in a well-appointed parlor decorated with a rug, an elaborate mirror, and curtains. Above the fireplace hangs a picture of a clergyman carrying a woman on his back to church. To the left Envy chases Truth and Justice out the open door. On the right two gentlemen peer into the room through an open window and listen to the ladies' conversation. The engraved lines below in verse berates women for their love of gossip and inability to follow the dictates of the ninth commandment, forbidding one to bear false witness against one's neighbor. To the left of the fireplace is a niche filled with cups, plates, and other tableware." I also note a tea board in the center of the table with tea cups, dishes, tea spoons on top of it. A ladies fan and what looks like a muff are also sitting on the table.

Tea Equipage

The tea table should be set as follows: the teacups on saucers are neatly arranged in a large semicircle around the teapot in the center (they can be right side up or upside down), flanked on one side by a bowl and on the other by a jug for milk or cream and a sugar container. Teaspoons are placed on the saucer or left in the cup. If a boat for teaspoon is a part of your tea set up, the teaspoons can be placed in a pile on the boat or just on the table. Tongs are best suited for lifting lumps of sugar from the container to the teacup. It is acceptable to use a cream pot of glass, pewter, or silver and burnt china. Milk pots are also used instead of cream if cream is unavailable in silver, pewter, ceramic, or sprig'd cut and moulded glass. All remaining tea and its dregs and particles are emptied into the slop bowl. (Roth)

Inventories

Inventories of the time also show the tea equipage in the homes of the colonists. It is interesting to note the inventories that I have found are from the very elite (i.e., Robert King Carter, Governor Eden) down to the middling classes (William Buckland), and show a range and variety of items owned for taking tea.

In the inventory of the personal estate of Robert King Carter of Virginia taken in November of 1733, it lists that he directed in his last Will the following tea items —

> "10 ditto Tea Cups & 8 Sawcers [sic]
> 1 Do. Small Dish
> I do. Teapott [sic] with a Silver Spout
> 2 Midling Cupps
> 1 Doz Earthen plates
> 5 Soop Do.
> 2 Copper Coffee potts

73

> 2 do. Tea Kettles…
> A box of Tea…
> 4 ditto Teapotts
> 2 Tea tables"

In Daniel Dulany's probate of May 1754, there was listed along with its value the following —

> 2 China Tea pots, 2 Canisters, 12 Cups, 12 Saucers 1. 5. 0
> One Set of China Containing One Tea Pot and Stand, 12 Cups and Saucers, 6 Coffee Cups, 1 Butter Plate, 1 Spoon Boat, 1 Bowl and Saucers, 1 Sugar Dish, 1 Cream Pot, 1 Canister 5.10. 0
> 3 old Tea Cups 9 Ditto Saucers and Tea Pot 1 Spoon Boat and 1 Stand . 2. 6
> One Set of Old Fashioned broken China on the Japan Tea Table contg 3 Tea pots, 3 Bowls 2 Butter Plates, 1 Stand, 1 Spoon Boat 1 Cream Pot, 7 Tea Cups, 8 Saucers & 11 Coffee Cups 1. 5.0
> 1 Tea Chest Silver Mounted 1.10. 0
> 1 [Silver] Tea Pot
> 1 Tea Pot
> 9 Tea Table Cloths 4.10. 0
> 5 Tea Table Cloths old 1. 0. 0
> 4 Tea Table Cloths very small . 8. 0
> 8 Tea napkins 9 old Do very small in all 17 .17. 0
> 2lb old Congo & 2 old Bohee Tea 1. 0. 0
> [white stone] Tea Cups and Saucers 1. 8. 1
> (Maryland State Archives)

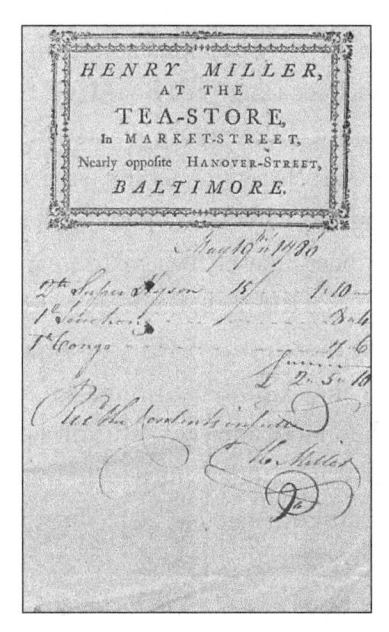

Henry Miller at the Tea Store, Baltimore, Winterthur

In a letter from London, Benjamin Franklin to his wife Deborah Franklin dated February 19, 1758, writes, among other news,

> "I send you by Capt. Budden, a large Case mark'd D.F. No. 1. and a small Box DF No. 2. In the large Case is another small Box, containing some English China; viz. Melons and Leaves for a Desert of Fruit and Cream, or the like; a Bowl remarkable for the Neatness of the Figures, made at Bow, near this City, some Coffee Cups of the same; a Worcester Bowl, ordinary. To show the Difference of Workmanship there is something from all the China Works in England; and one old true China Bason mended, of an odd Colour. The same Box contains 4 Silver Salt Ladles, newest, but ugliest, Fashion; a little Instrument to Core Apples; another to make little Turnips out of great ones; Six coarse diaper Breakfast Cloths; they are to spread on the

Tea Table, for no body breakfasts here on the naked Table, but on the Cloth set a large Tea Board with the Cups; there is also a little Basket, a Present from Mrs. Stephenson to Sally, and a Pair of Garters for you which were knit by the young Lady her Daughter, who favour'd me with a Pair of the same kind, the only ones I have been able to wear; as they need not be bound tight, the Ridges in them preventing their Slipping. We send them therefore as a Curiosity for the Form, more than for the Value. Goody Smith may, if she pleases, make such for me hereafter, and they will suit her own fat Knees. My Love to her." (Founders, https://founders.archives.gov/documents/Franklin/01-07-02-0163)

Mentioned in the book *Notes and Documents, Henry Bouquet: His Relict Possessions* by Douglas E. Branch states that Brigadier General Henry Bouquet, who passed away while he commanded the forces in the "Southern District" at Fort St. George, Pensacola, owned several tea related items. The inventory of his effects dated September 4, 1765 included "1 small tea pott, 1 milk pott, 1 tea tongues, 1 copper tea kettle, 2 cannisters tea, 2 tea kettles, and two drinking cups."

Mrs. Henrietta Maria Dulany's probate in November 1766, Annapolis, Maryland included —

> Mahogony Tea Table 1.15. 0
> 1 Mahogany Tea Chest & Canesters . 9. 0
> 1 very old Japand Table & Tea Bord . 4. 0
> 1 Mahogany Tea Waiter . 8. 0
> 1 Mahogany Tea Table Broke 1. 5. 0
> 1 Mahogany Tea bord .12. 6
> 1 tea Chest Silver Mounted 1.15. 0
> A Set of Tin Canesters for a Tea Chest . 3. 6
> 5 lb fine Hyson Tea in Canesters 22/ 5.10. 0

1 lb Sanisong tea .12. 0
3 Tea Kettles 1. 0. 0
1 Mahogany Tea Chest & Canesters . 9. 0

John Brice — probate Annapolis May 1767
Tea 30/ (in store)
8 Tea Kittles 90/ (in store)
Tea Board 2/
hand and Tea Board 14/6
3lb Congo Tea 42/
3½ Bohea Tea 21/
2 Tea Chests 20/
2 Tea Kittles 15/
(Maryland State Archives)

The infamous architect, William Buckland's probate in Annapolis, Maryland of December 1774 included —

One Mahoghany Tea Table 1. 4. 0
Two Tea Kettles and Coffee pott.12. 0
One Mahogany Tea chest .10. 0
(Maryland State Archives)

Maryland's Governor Robert Eden left Virginia on the transport ship Levant on August 6, 1776 for Portsmouth arriving in London in September. His house inventory was taken in June of 1776 and the contents were left in the possession of His Excellency Thomas Sim Lee Esq. and included the following with their values —

1 Carved claw and pillar tea table £3.10.0
3 Tea boards £2.5.0
11 Silver tea spoons & 2 pair tea tongs £5.0.0

9 Blue and white tea cups and saucers £0.15.0
5 China teapots £0.15.0
4 Tea kettles £2.0.0
1 Japanned tea kitchen £1.0.0
(Maryland State Archives)

The inventory of John Carlyle of Fairfax, Virginia in 1780 and recorded in 1783 included—

"…one painted Tea Table, 7 tea spoons, 2 China Tea pots, 6 China cups and saucers different patrons, old carved mahogany tea table & board, 1 Silver tea pot, cream pot, broken sugar tongs, 2 China Tea Canisters one without a top, 1 China Sugar dish Cracked, 1 China Tea Pott Stand, 1 Copper Tea Kittle, 1 Large Tea Cannister, 1 old Tea Board, 1 pair Tongs…" (Fairfax County Will Book)

General Washington writes from Rocky Hill on September 22, 1783, to his brother Bushrod, "There is another thing likewise which I wish to know, without having it known for whom the enquiry is made; and that is, whether French plate is fashionable and much used in genteel houses in France and England; and whether, as we have heard, the quantity in Philadelphia is large, of what pieces it consists, and whether among them, there are Tea urns, Coffee pots, Tea pots, and other equipage for a tea table, with a tea board, Candlesticks and waiters large and small, with the prices of each. These enquiries you may make in behalf of a friend, without bringing my name forward, 'till occasion (if a purchase shou'd happen) may require it." (GW Papers at the Library of Congress)

In 1799, George Washington passed away and the inventory of his estate, which included all of his farms, was recorded in Fairfax County. The items that specifically mentioned "tea" include "3 tea tables, 1 tea pot, 1

Tea Equipage

Egyptian China Pot, 1 Plated Tea board, 1 tea urn, 2 cream dishes, 2 sugar dishes, 1 Cream Pott, 1 Tea Urn. (GW Papers at the Library of Congress)

> WILLIAMSBURG, *August* 7, 1777.
>
> TO BE SOLD, and entered on immediately, a valuable House on the Market Square in this City, with 4 handsome Rooms below neatly papered, and a Fire Place in each, with 3 Closets, and 6 Rooms above, with dry Cellars under the Whole, a good Kitchen and Laundry, with Closets, a Brick Dairy, Corn House, Smokehouse, Stable, and Coach Houses, with a Flower and Kitchen Garden, well paled in; also a small House adjoining, with 2 Rooms and Fire Places, a good Cellar, and Yard, the Whole in good Repair. With the above Houses may be had, all or any Part of the following valuable Furniture, *viz.* Mahogany Dining Tables, Pembrook, Card, Toilet, and other Tables, large and small handsome Looking Glasses, an eight Day Clock, Mahogany Chairs, with Brocade, and Furniture Bottoms, green Passage Chairs, Carpets, and Carpeting, a large Mahogany Plate Case, with Glass Doors, a Mahogany Bureau, on Brass Castors, a Tea Urn with a Mahogany Stand, Beds, Bedsteads, and Curtains, Tea, and Table China, Bowls, and ornamental China, japanned, Glass, and Queen's Ware, a Brass Grate, a Bath Stove, Handirons, Brass and Wire Fenders, a good Jack, and a Quantity of Kitchen Furniture, also a large imported Flour Mill, with a Variety of other Articles too tedious to mention. The Terms may be known by applying to the Subscriber, on the Premises, who intends leaving this State in a short Time, and requests those who have any Claims against him immediately to apply for Payment, and all who are indebted to him, either by Bond or Account, will be so good to discharge their several Balances as soon as possible.
>
> JOHN BAKER.

Virginia Gazette, August 8, 1777

CHAPTER 6

Receipts with or to Take with Tea

First, we must discuss how to read an 18th century recipe, or what they called a "receipt." In today's society, everyone seems to want recipes that are easy and quick to make that have very few or detailed steps in which to do so. In a world of frozen, canned, ready-made meals, and fast food it is easy to go with that route. Why wouldn't we? We have progressed to the point where we don't have to cook if we do not want to.

In the 18th century, it wasn't possible to walk into a grocery store to buy stock for a stew. You (or servants) made the stock. Growing the items you needed to make it and the intended dish were the way it was done. For those who lived in cities, it was possible to purchase items at the market which was often held on a specific street with vendors hawking their wares.

Everything was grown seasonally or required preparation by someone. Our ready-made foods are made for us today. In the time, a tavern or inn also offered food for sale for travelers and locals alike.

The idea of cooking from scratch can seem daunting, but there are some common sense ways in which to make the receipts of the time in ours.

When first going through original receipts, read them through a few times and then —

Receipts with or to Take with Tea

- Write down the ingredients and measurements. If not in terms you understand, refer to the chapter in this book on measurements to convert them.
- Figure out if you need to make something required in the receipt before you start it. If you do, can you substitute it with something you can buy today? If not, where do you find out how to make it? (I first refer to my other book, *A Book of Cookery by a Lady*, and if not there, I look at historic cookery books of the time to find it.) In some cases, ingredients can be left out.
- Figure out how it will be cooked and what equipment is needed to do that. Will you make it over a fire, on your stove, or in your oven at home? Do you need a bowl or utensils to put it together? Do you need to cook part of it first? What do you need to cook it in? Do you need to pre-heat anything?

This book includes two chapters on measurements and cooking terms from *A Book of Cookery, by a Lady* that you can refer to. I have also made notes at the end of each receipt to assist. All receipts are sourced so you know exactly where I found them. Additionally, many are similar or almost the same, and the names changed. There was no copyright until the early 20th century.

Virginia Gazette, 27 September 1776

Medicinal

Some of these receipts that included tea were for medicinal use and are not recommended for use today. There are others that called it "tea" when there is no actual tea in it. I'm including these verbatim as they were written to relieve or cure certain ailments. When in doubt, do not make these to consume or use.

The Poor Richard's Almanac in 1740 recommends in "Dr. Tennent's infallible Cure for the Pleurisy" the following that includes a type of tea made from Marsh Mallard Roots and thyme or marjoram. Dr. Tennent says —

> "For ordinary Drink, give Hysop Decoction, or a Tea drawn from Marsh Mallard Roots, sweetned with Honey; but in case of a Purging attending the Case, let the Drink be sweetned with double refined Sugar, and the Cinnamon and Harts Horn before prescribed are to be given with the poudered Rattlesnake Root in a little of it; and it is to be observed, that both the Decoction of the Root and Tea are given warm. If the Patient be troubled with a Vomiting, or Nausea, give one spoonful and half of the Decoction every three Hours, or if that should immediately be thrown up, give half a spoonful of the Decoction every Hour; observing in such a Case to bleed, as before advised. There is a Disease called a Pleurisy, wherein Bleeding is of ill Consequence, which may with great Propriety be called a latent or spurious Peripneumony; yet the above Method with the Decoction of the Root, is a very certain one, giving instead of pectoral Teas, a Tea made of Thyme or Marjoram, or rather Rum-punch." (Founders, https://founders.archives.gov/documents/Franklin/01-02-02-0053)

NOTE: Hyssop is native to the Mediterranean and Asia and of the mint family. The leaves/stems can be made into a decoction or oil and used for various conditions. Marshmallow leaf and root is a plant, also used in medicines. Harts Horn is the horn of a red male deer. Rattlesnake Root is a plant from the Prenanthes family with bitter tasting tuberous roots and white to purple nodding flower heads.

Sage Tea

TAKE a little sage, a little balm, put it into a pan, slice a lemon, peel and all, a few knobs of sugar one glass of white wine; pour on these two or three quarts of boiling water; cover it, and drink when thirsty. When you think it strong enough of the herbs take them out, otherwise it will make it bitter. (Briggs)

NOTE: When "taking a little" sage or balm (lemon balm of the mint family) means it is a judgement measurement as to how strong you want the drink to be. In this case, two or three quarts will make quite a bit which was not meant to drink all at once, but to "drink when thirsty," so there was some left over and stored. You will want enough sage and balm to give it flavor. A knob is a lump and can equate to being one or two tablespoons. In the time period, sugar was made into a large cone and processed/refined. Using sugar tongs, you would break off pieces or lumps to put into your sugar bowl or receipt. It may be easier if you cut the receipt in half and make a smaller batch.

Tea Caudle

MAKE a quart of strong green Tea, and pour it out into a skillet, and set it over the fire; then beat the yolks of four eggs, and mix with them a pint of white-wine, a grated nutmeg, sugar to your taste, and put all together; stir it over the fire till 'tis very hot, then drink it in China dishes as caudle.

NOTE: The John Ash Dictionary of 1775 defined a caudle as "a mixture of wine and other ingredients." (Smith)

Eggs

An egg broken into a cup of tea, or beaten and mixed with a basin of milk, makes a breakfast more supporting than tea solely. (Rundell 1814)

NOTE: This is basically a cup of your choice of tea that has a beaten egg and milk added to it.

A Refreshing Drink in a Fever

Put a little tea-sage, two sprigs of balm, and a little sorrel, into a stone jug, having first washed and dried them; peel thin a small lemon, and clear from the white; slice it, and put a bit of the peel in; then pour in three pints of boiling water, sweeten, and cover it close. (Rundell 1814)

NOTE: This receipt basically has sage, lemon balm, sorrel, lemon, sugar, and water. It tells you to wash the sage, lemon balm, and sorrel before use. Then peel a small lemon and take out the white (or pith). Take the lemon peel and put it with the sage, lemon balm, and sorrel in a stone jug (or vessel you want). Boil three pints of water on the stove or fire and then put it in the jug with the ingredients and sweeten to taste. Ensure that the vessel you use will not crack when boiling water is put into it. Sorrel is a perennial herb used in salads.

For the Gout

MAKE a Conserve of Buck-bean, with the weight in Sugar-candy; beat both fine, and take as much as a large Nutmeg, first and last; and drink a Tea made of the same Herb every Morning and Afternoon, constantly, for one whole Year. This alone, without any, other Medicine, made a perfect: Cure in a Person that had been many Years most grievously afflicted; and is effectual in the *Scurvy*, or *Rheumatick Pains*. Where the Patient is Weak, and very Restless, 'tis best to mix a third-part Venice Treacle in the Conserve they take when going to Rest. (For the Use of All Good Wives…)

NOTE: This receipt tells you to make a conserve or jam made from the leaves of Buck-bean, also known as bogbean from the Menyanthaceae

Receipts with or to Take with Tea

family, with sugar candy and nutmeg. Sugar candy is crystalized sugar or essentially rock sugar. Mithridatium or Theriac is "Venice Treacle" — an ancient panacea that would not be a remedy today as it uses a viper and other ingredients.

For a Cough
MAKE a strong Tea of Ale-hoof, sweeten it with Sugar-candy, and drink it First and Last. (For the Use of All Good Wives…)

NOTE: Ale-hoof is ground ivy. Sugar-candy is crystalized sugar or essentially rock sugar. English ivy is used now to make medicines, and supposedly helps with congestion in the lungs.

For the Rheumatism
Take a Quart of Anniseed, Half an Ounce of Rhubarb sliced, and two Pounds of Raisins stoned. Drink a Glass of this nine Mornings together. Or, Drink Buckbane Tea every Morning, with two Tea-Spoonfuls of Hartshorn Drops. This has cured a thousand poor People, and why not the Rich? (Harrison)

NOTE: Rheumatism is achy joints and muscles. Today we can purchase raisins without seeds so do not need to remove their "stones." Buckbane is buck-bean or bogbean as described in the "For the Grout" receipt. Hartshorn is the antlers of red male deer boiled down and used for baking, as smelling salts, oil, or as jelly (gelatin).

For the Rheumatism
Take two Spoonfuls of Linseed-Oil made without Fire; take it in the Morning fasting, and as much before going to Bed, for nine Days together, and keep yourself very warm. (Harrison)

NOTE: This is another receipt for achy joints and muscles, and has you take two spoonfuls of flaxseed oil. Flaxseed oil is safe to ingest. Two spoonfuls are tablespoons.

To Cure the Flux

Take the Stalks and Leaves of Fleabane, dry them gently, and powder them. Of this Powder give about a Drachm at a Time, in Green Tea or Broth, twice in a Day. (Harrison)

NOTE: Fleabane is a part of the daisy family. It is considered toxic and should not be ingested. It was put in tea or broth to cure the diarrhea or dysentery. A Drachm is 1/8th of a fluid ounce.

Receipt for the Gout and Rheumatism

Take Aristolochia and Gentian Roots, Germander, Ground Pine, and Centaury, Tops and Leaves, dry'd, powder'd, and sifted as fine as you can, of each equal Quantities. The Dose is a Drachm in a Morning fasting in Wine and Water, Tea, or any other Vehicle, for three Months; three Quarters of a Drachm for three Months shore; Half a Drachm for three Months more; and then Half a Drachm every other Day for a Twelvemonth. To be taken in the Fit as well as out of the Fit. Forbear high Sauces, Drams, Champagne, &c. and use moderate Exercise, particularly Riding. (Harrison)

NOTE: Tea was used in this instance as a means to take a medicine. Aristolochia is used today to treat gout and achy joints and muscles (or rheumatism). Gentian is an herb and is not recommended for use unless fully researched. Germander is a plant that is part of the mint, lavender, and salvia family. Ground pine is also a flowering plant of the mint family.

Beef Tea

Cut a pound of fleshy beef in thin slices; simmer with a quart of water twenty minutes, after it has once boiled, and been skimmed. Season, if approved; but it has generally only salt. (Rundell)

NOTE: This is self-explanatory in that it is essentially beef broth.

Receipts with or to Take with Tea

For Breakfast and to take with the Tea Ceremony

The Best Receipt for Ginger Bread
"3 lb of flour, 1 oz of sugar, a very full pint of molasses, ½ a pound of butter (which must be creamed in winter) and a ¼ oz nice lard, ginger to your tast[e]. Stir the molasses butter & sugar well together, in the first place, then work in the flour by degrees, it requires a little over the 3 lb to make it of a consistence to roll, but it must by no means be stiff." (Carroll)

NOTE: The receipt is pretty explanatory, and may need to be cut by a half or thirds. Try using lard, but if you cannot find it, use Crisco. It also does not tell you how to bake it. Depending on how much batter you have, choose a loaf pan, and bake it at a moderate heat (or 325 to 350 degrees) until done or a knife comes out clean when you put it into the center.

Light Cake
"4 lbs of flour, a lb and ¼ oz. of sugar — a lb of butter, 8 eggs leaving out 4 whites, a gill of wine — a pint of new milk, a pint of yeast — one of nutmeg a desert spoonful of mace, and a large one of cinnamon — time will bake them." (Carroll)

NOTE: This receipt can be reduced in half. A desert spoonful was meant to be a "dessert" spoonful and would be two teaspoon. This receipt also does not tell you what to use or how to bake it. Use a round cake pan, and bake it at a moderate heat. A "lb" is a pound.

Tea Custard
"Receits kept by Mary Booth, daughter of the 2d Early of Warrington: "Take a pint and a half of cream, eight eggs leaving out the whites: beat your eggs very well and put about half your cream to them, and as much sugar as you think will sweaten it. Then take the other half of your cream with about half an ounce of your finest green tea, and stew them together until you think you have got all the flavor and colour of the tea. Then strain through a lawn sieve in the other half of your cream and eggs; stir it over

a slow fire until it grows thick: keep it stirring 'till it is almost cold, then pour it into your dish and serve it up. If you have any Naples Biscuits, you may ornament it at top in flowers or as you please. You may if you like it, colour with Pastatichio Nuts or spinage juice [sic], but it is reckon'd better without." (Pettigrew & Richardson)

NOTE: A lawn sieve is a piece of fine linen fabric. Straining it with linen will get the tea leaves out of it. You can make it this way, or put your tea in a linen bag or use tea bags to skip this step. Coloring it with Pistachios or spinach juice was meant to turn it green. Naples biscuits are a flour, sugar, and egg "cookie" in whatever shape you like, and often flavored with rose or orange flower water. There is a receipt for Naples Biscuit in this book.

To Make Tea Crumpets

BEAT two eggs very, well, put to them a quart of warm milk and water, and a large spoonful of barm; beat in as much fine flour as will make them rather thicker than a common batter pudding, then make your bake-stone very hot, and rub it with a little butter wrapped in a clean linen cloth, then pour a large spoonful of batter upon your stone, and let it run to the size of a tea saucer; turn it, and when you want to use them toast them very crisp and butter them. (Raffald)

Note: Barm is the foam formed on the top of the liquid used, normally beer or wine, when fermenting to make bread. You can use dry yeast as a substitute. A large spoonful is a tablespoon full. These are very like a pancake, and if they go cold you can toast them and serve. You can use a baking stone or a baking tray.

Buckwheat Cakes

TAKE a quart of buckwheat meal, mix with it a tea-spoonful of salt, and add a handful of Indian meal. Pour a large table-spoonful of the best brewer's yeast into the centre of the meal. Then mix it gradually with cold water till it becomes a batter. Cover it, put it in a warm place and set it to rise; it will take about three hours. When it is quite light, and covered

Receipts with or to Take with Tea

with bubbles, it is fit to bake. Put your griddle over the fire, and let it get quite hot before you begin. Grease it well with a piece of butter tied in a rag. Then dip out a large ladle full of the batter and bake it on the griddle; turning it with a broad wooden paddle. Let the cakes be of large size, and even at the edges. Ragged edges to batter cakes look very badly. Butter them as you take them off the griddle. Put several on a plate, and cut them across in six pieces. Grease the griddle anew, between baking each cake. If your batter has been mixed overnight and is found to be sour in the morning, melt in warm water a piece of pearl-ash the size of a grain of corn, or a little larger; stir it into the batter; let it set half an hour, and then bake it. The pearl-ash will remove the sour taste, and increase the lightness of the cakes. (Leslie)

NOTE: Buckwheat meal can be purchased today as Buckwheat flour. It is gluten free. Indian meal is ground corn meal. Pearl-ash is potassium carbonate or what we know today as baking soda. Use ½ teaspoon for every teaspoon of pearl-ash called for.

Fallel Cakes

Put a table-spoonful of butter into a quart of milk and warm them together till the butter has melted; then stir it well, and set it away too cool. Beat five eggs as light as possible, and stir them into the milk in turn with three pints of sifted flour; add a small tea-spoonful of salt, and a large table-spoonful and a half of the best fresh yeast. Set the pan of batter near the fire to rise; and if the yeast is good, it will be light in three hours. Then bake it on a griddle in the manner of buckwheat cakes. Send them to table hot, and cut across into four pieces. This batter may be baked in waffle-irons. If so, send to table with the cakes powdered white sugar and cinnamon. (Leslie)

NOTE: You can use dry brewer's yeast for this. You can use a modern waffle maker for this, or an antique one over the fire.

Indian Batter Cakes

Mix together a quart of sifted Indian meal (the yellow meal is best for all purposes), and a handful of wheat flour. Warm a quart of milk, and stir into it a small tea-spoonful of salt, and two large table-spoonfuls of the best fresh yeast. Beat three eggs very light, and stir them gradually into the milk in turn with the meal. Cover it, and set it to rise for three or four hours. When quite light, bake it on a griddle in the manner of buckwheat cakes. Butter them, cut them across, and send them to table hot, with molasses in a sauce-boat. If the batter should chance to become sour before it is baked, stir in about a salt-spoonful of pearl-ash dissolved in a little lukewarm water; and let it set half an hour longer before it is baked. (Leslie)

NOTE: Indian meal is ground corn meal. Pearl-ash is potassium carbonate or what we know today as baking soda. Use ½ teaspoon for every teaspoon of pearl-ash called for.

Indian Mush Cakes

Pour into a pan three pints of cold water, and stir gradually into it a quart of sifted Indian meal which has been mixed with half a pint of wheat flour, and a small tea-spoonful of salt. Give it a hard stirring at the last. Have ready a hot griddle, and bake the batter immediately, in cakes about the size of a saucer. Send them to table piled evenly, but not cut. Eat them with butter or molasses. This is the most economical and expeditious way of making soft; but it cannot be recommended as the best. It will be some improvement to mix the meal with milk rather than water. (Leslie)

NOTE: These are similar to those eaten by George Washington for breakfast with honey. Margaret Carroll also had a receipt called "a nice kind of breakfast cake" below.

A Nice Kind of Breakfast Cake

Take 3 pints of fine flour or ground seconds, and 1 pint of Indian meal, with about 1-1/2 spoonful of yeast — mix all well together, to the consistence of a batter for pancakes — let it stand all night to lighten — and bake them on a very hot griddle. (Carroll)

NOTE: "Ground seconds" is a coarser ground flour such as a stone ground coarse wheat flour. Indian meal is ground corn meal.

Johnny Cake

Sift a quart of Indian meal into a pan; make a hole in the middle, and pour in a pint of warm water. Mix the meal and water gradually into a batter, adding a small tea-spoonful of salt. Beat it very hard, and for a long time, till it becomes quite light. Then spread it thick and even on a stout piece of smooth board. Place it upright on the hearth before a clear fire, with a flat iron or something of the sort to support the board behind, and bake it well. Cut it into squares, and split and butter them hot. (Leslie)

NOTE: Indian meal is ground corn meal.

Indian Flappers

Have ready a pint of sifted Indian meal, mixed with a handful of wheat flour, and a small tea-spoonful of salt. Beat four eggs very light, and stir them by degrees into a quart of milk, in turn with the meal. They can be made in a very short time, and should be baked as soon as mixed, on a hot griddle; allow a large ladle full of batter to each cake, and make them all of the same size. Send them to table hot, buttered and cut in half. (Leslie)

NOTE: Indian meal is ground corn meal.

Indian Muffins

Sift and mix together a pint and a half of yellow Indian meal, and a handful of wheat flour. Melt a quarter of a pound of fresh butter in a quart of milk. Beat four eggs very light, and stir into them alternately (a little at a time of each) the milk when it is quite cold, and the meal; adding a small tea-spoonful of salt. The whole must be beaten long and hard. Then butter some muffin rings; set them on a hot griddle, and pour some of the batter into each. Send the muffins to table hot, and split them by pulling them open with your fingers, as a knife will make them heavy. Eat them with butter, molasses or honey. (Leslie)

NOTE: Indian meal is ground corn meal. Muffin rings are available today and look very like a cookie cutter. A muffin pan could also be used.

Water Muffins

Put four table-spoonfuls of fresh strong yeast into a pint of lukewarm water. Add a little salt; about a small tea-spoonful; then stir in gradually as much sifted flour as will make a thick batter. Cover the pan, and set it in a warm place to rise. When it is quite light, and your griddle is hot, grease and set your muffin rings on it; having first buttered them round the inside. Dip out a ladle full of the batter for each ring, and bake them over a quick fire. Send them to table hot, and split them by pulling them open with your hands. (Leslie)

NOTE: A quick fire is 400 degrees F in the oven.

Common Muffins

Having melted three table-spoonfuls of butter in three pints of warm milk, set it away to cool. Then beat three eggs as light as possible, and stir them gradually into the milk when it is quite cold; adding a tea-spoonful of salt. Stir in by degrees enough of sifted flour to make a batter as thick as you can conveniently beat it; and lastly, add two table-spoonfuls of strong fresh yeast from the brewery. Cover the batter and set it in a warm place to rise. It should be light in about three hours. Having heated your griddle, grease it with some butter tied in a rag; grease your muffin rings round the inside, and set them on the griddle. Take some batter out of the pan with a ladle or a large spoon, pour it lightly into the rings, and bake the muffins of a light brown. When done, break or split them open with your fingers; butter them and send them to table hot. (Leslie)

NOTE: You can use dry brewer's yeast in place of the "fresh yeast."

Receipts with or to Take with Tea

Soda Biscuits

Melt half a pound of butter in a pint of warm milk, adding a tea-spoonful of soda; and stir in by degrees half a pound of sugar. Then sift into a pan two pounds of flour; make a hole in the middle; pour in the milk, &c., and mix it with the flour into a dough. Put it on your paste-board, and knead it long and hard till it becomes very light. Roll it out into a sheet half an inch thick. Cut it into little round cakes with the top of a wine glass, or with a tin cutter of that size; prick the tops; lay them on tins sprinkled with flour, or in shallow iron pans; and bake them of a light brown in a quick oven; they will be done in a few minutes. These biscuits keep very well. (Leslie)

NOTE: "Soda" is probably Pearl-ash. Pearl-ash is potassium carbonate or what we know today as baking soda. Use ½ teaspoon for every teaspoon of pearl-ash called for.

A Sally Lunn

This cake is called after the inventress. Sift into a pan a pound and a half of flour. Make a hole in the middle, and put in two ounces of butter warmed in a pint of milk, a salt-spoonful of salt, three well-beaten eggs, and two table-spoonfuls of the best fresh yeast. Mix the flour well into the other ingredients, and put the whole into a square tin pan that has been greased with butter. Cover it, set it in a warm place, and when it is quite light, bake it in a moderate oven. Send it to table hot, and eat it with butter. Or, you may bake it on a griddle, in small muffin rings, pulling the cakes open and buttering them when brought to table. (Leslie)

NOTE: You can use brewer's yeast for the "best fresh yeast." A moderate oven is 350-400 degree Fahrenheit.

Short Cakes

Rub three quarters of a pound of fresh butter into a pound and a half of sifted flour; and make it into a dough with a little cold water. Roll it out into a sheet half an inch thick, and cut it into round cakes with the edge of a tumbler. Prick them with a fork; lay them in a shallow iron pan sprinkled with flour, and bake them in a moderate oven till they are brown. Send them to table hot; split and butter them. (Leslie)

NOTE: A tumbler is a drinking glass. Rubbing butter into flour means the butter should be cold. You can use your hands to rub the butter and flour together being careful not to warm it too much as you want the mixture to be crumbly. Or, as I like to do, use two knives to cut the butter into the flour which achieves the same result without warming it.

Tea Biscuits

Melt a quarter of a pound of fresh butter in a quart of warm milk, and add a salt-spoonful of salt. Sift two pounds of flour into a pan, make a hole in the centre, and put in three table-spoonfuls of the best brewer's yeast. Add the milk and butter and mix it into a stiff paste. Cover it and set it by the fire to rise. When quite light, knead it well, roll it out an inch thick, and cut it into round cakes with the edge of a tumbler. Prick the top of each with a fork; lay them in buttered pans and bake them light brown. Send them to table warm, and split and butter them. (Leslie)

NOTE: A salt-spoonful is about 1/4 teaspoon. You can use dry brewer's yeast for this.

How to Make Naples Biscuit

Take a pound of fine sugar and three quarters of the finest flour you can get; the sugar must be finely seered, and the flour three times; then add six eggs beat very well, and two or three grains of musk with a spoonful of rose water; heat your oven, and when it is almost hot make them, taking care they be not made up wet. (Glasse)

NOTE: The musk in this recipe is from a deer, and were glandular secretions. It is best to just use rose water to flavor your batter. I have found that a later rendition of this receipt is easier to use and more tasty. *The Virginia Housewife* states to beat twelve eggs light, add to them one pound of flour, and one of powdered sugar; continue to beat all together till perfectly light; bake it in long pans, four inches wide, with divisions; so that each cake, when done, will be four inches long, and one and a half wide.

Rice Cakes

Pick and wash half a pint of rice, and boil it very soft. Then drain it, and let it get cold. Sift a pint and a half of flour over the pan of rice, and mix in a quarter of a pound of butter that has been warmed by the fire, and a salt-spoonful of salt. Beat five eggs very light, and stir them gradually into a quart of milk. Beat the whole very hard, and bake it in muffin rings, or in waffle-irons. Send them to table hot, and eat them with butter, honey, or molasses. You may make these cakes of rice flour instead of mixing together whole rice and wheat flour. (Leslie)

NOTE: This is a confusing receipt, but reading it a couple of times will allow you to figure it out. This is how I read it — Wash the rice in cold water, put it in a pan and boil it in water until soft, and set aside. Beat five eggs into a quart of milk. Pre-heat a frying pan, add the butter and salt, after the butter has melted, add the rice, stir it, and then sift wheat flour over it, all the while continuing to stir. When it is all mixed, take it off the fire. You can then use the batter to pour into muffin rings/pan to bake, or put into a waffle maker. Eat with butter, honey, or molasses. The receipt says you can substitute rice flour instead of using whole rice. I'd also consider using jam or jelly on these.

Cream Cakes

Having three eggs very light, stir them into a quart of cream alternately with a quart of sifted flour; and add one wine glass of strong yeast, and a salt-spoon of salt. Cover the batter, and set it near the fire to rise. When it is quite light, stir in a large table-spoonful of butter that has been warmed by the fire. Bake the cakes in muffin rings, and send them to table hot, split with your fingers, and buttered. (Leslie)

NOTE: This receipt should probably be cut into ½ or thirds.

French Rolls

Sift a pound of flour into a pan, and rub into it two ounces of butter; mix in the whites only of three eggs, beaten to a stiff froth, and a table-spoonful of strong yeast; add sufficient milk to make a stiff dough, and a salt-spoonful of salt. Cover it and set it before the fire to rise. It should be light in an hour. Then put it on a paste-board, divide it into rolls, or round cakes; lay them in a floured square pan, and bake them about ten minutes in a quick oven. (Leslie)

NOTE: This is similar to how we make bread from scratch today (outside of the machines). When using yeast, determine how much you need based upon the suggested amounts of the yeast. "It should be light in an hour" means it should rise and be ready to divide up.

Common Rolls

Sift two pounds of flour into a pan, and mix with it a tea-spoonful of salt. Warm together a jill of water and a jill of milk. Make a hole in the middle of the pan of flour; mix with the milk and water a jill of the best yeast, and pour it into the hole. Mix into the liquid enough of the surrounding flour to make a thin batter, which you must stir till quite smooth and free from lumps. Then strew a handful of flour over the top, and set it in a warm place to rise for two hours or more. When it is quite light, and has cracked on the top, make it into a dough with some more milk and water. Knead it well for ten minutes. Cover it, and set it again to rise for twenty minutes. Then make the dough into rolls or round balls. Bake them in a square pan, and send them to table hot, cut in three, buttered and put together again. (Leslie)

NOTE: A jill is a gill. The pan you put the flour in can also be a paste board or a pan big enough for you to mix it.

Tea Cakes

Rub fine four ounces of butter into eight ounces of flour; mix eight ounces of currants, and six of fine Lisbon sugar, two yolks and one white of eggs, and a spoonful of brandy. Roll the paste the thickness of an Oliver biscuit, and cut with a wine glass. You may beat the other white, and wash over them; and either dust sugar, or not, as you like. (Rundell)

NOTE: Lisbon sugar is a double refined off-white sugar. An Oliver biscuit is named after William Oliver who coined the name in 1750. They are a very thin, hard, dry cracker/cookie/biscuit often eaten with cheese. These are a sweet cracker of the day. You can leave out the currants if they are not to your taste.

Tea Cakes

One pound sugar, half pound butter, two pound flour, three eggs, one gill yeast, a little cinnamon and orange peel; bake fifteen minutes. (simmons)

NOTE: This receipt leaves out a lot of things, but sounds wonderful. These would be made into either little cakes, or could be put in muffin rings and baked.

Benton Tea Cakes

Mix a paste of flour, a little bit of butter, and milk: roll as thin as possible, and bake on a back-stone over the fire, or on a hot hearth. (Rundell)

NOTE: This essentially says that your flour, butter, and milk would mix into a paste. Note it does not call for sugar. Try it this way the first time and adapt to your taste.

Another sort, as Biscuits

Run into a pound of flour six ounces of butter, and three large spoonfuls of yeast, and make into a paste, with a sufficient quantity of new milk; make into biscuits, and prick them with a clean fork. (Rundell)

NOTE: New milk is fresh milk. Bake them in a moderate oven.

Another Sort

Melt six or seven ounces of butter with a sufficiency of new milk warmed to make seven pounds of flour into a stiff paste; roll thin, and make into biscuits. (Rundell)

NOTE: This makes a LOT of biscuits. It could be cut into half or thirds. You will also want to bake it in a moderate oven.

A Biscuit Cake

One pound of flour, five eggs well beaten and strained, eight ounces of sugar, a little rose, or orange-flower water beat the whole thoroughly, and bake one hour. (Rundell)

NOTE: Bake in a moderate oven in a shallow round cake pan.

Macaroons

Blanch four ounces of almonds, and pound with four spoonfuls of orange-flower water; whisk the whites of four eggs to a froth, then mix it, and a pound of sugar, sifted, with the almonds, to a paste; and laying a sheet of wafer-paper on a tin, put it on in different little cakes, the shape of macaroons. (Rundell)

NOTE: This calls for powdered almonds which can be purchased today if you do not want to go through grinding them up. A food processor could also grind them up. Add orange-flower water to four egg whites beaten to a froth. Use baking paper on a cookie sheet. You can use cookie cutters to make various shapes. The shape of a macaroon was a little long roll. This is not to be confused with the macaron or coconut macaroon of today.

Wafers

Dry the flour well which you intend to use, mix a little pounded sugar and finely-pounded mace with it; then make it into a thick batter with cream; butter the wafer irons, let them be hot; put a tea-spoonful of the batter into them, so bake them carefully, and roll them off the iron with a stick. (Rundell)

NOTE: You can use wafer irons if cooking over a fire, or a pizzelle maker if at home. You can use powered mace, always use sparingly and add to taste.

Crack Nuts

Mix eight ounces of flour, and eight ounces of sugar; melt four ounces of butter in two spoonfuls of raisin wine; then, with four eggs beaten and strained, make into paste; add caraways, roll out as thin as paper, cut with the top of a glass, wash with the white of an egg, and dust sugar over. (Rundell)

NOTE: Raisin wine is also known as Straw wine. Raisin wine is made from grapes that have been dried or hung in the sun. You can purchase or make your own. These have an egg white wash and coating of sugar on them before and after baking.

Cracknels

Mix with a quart of flour half a nutmeg grated, the yolks of four eggs beaten, with four spoonfuls of rose-water, into a stiff paste, with cold water; then roll in a pound of butter, and make them into a cracknel shape; put them into a kettle of boiling water, and boil them till they swim, then take out, and put them into cold water; when hardened, lay them out to dry, and bake them on tin plates. (Rundell)

NOTE: Per the John Ash Dictionary, Volume 1, of 1775 — a cracknel is a hard brittle kind of cake. Cracknel comes from crack which states that it is "breaking by which the parts are separated but a little way from each other." Cake is also defined as "any mass of matter rather wide than high." So I would make up little flat round disks — any size you like — and boil them like noodles — when they start to float, take them out and let them dry. Then bake. Try it this way, try them just boiled, and try them just baked and see what you like.

A Good Plain bun, that may be eaten with or without toasting and butter

Rub four ounces of butter into two pounds of flour, four ounces of sugar, a nutmeg, or not, as you like, a few Jamaica peppers, a desert spoonful of caraways; put a spoonful or two of cream into a cup of yeast, and as much good milk as will make the above into a light paste. Set it to rise by a fire till the oven be ready. They will quickly bake on tins. (Rundell)

NOTE: Jamaica peppers equates to allspice today. A "desert" spoon is a dessert spoon or 2 teaspoonsful.

Richer Buns

Mix one pound and a half of dried flour with half a pound of sugar; melt a pound and two ounces of butter in a little warm water; add six spoonfuls of rose-water, and knead the above into a light dough, with half a pint of yeast; then mix five ounces of caraway-comfits in, and put some on them. (Rundell)

NOTE: A comfit is a sweetmeat also known as a sucket. So the caraway comfit would be a sugared caraway seed. Candying or conserving (to candy or pickle) in the time would mean rolling or rubbing the seed multiple times (based upon how much sugar you want on them) in sugar to encrust it. Allow them to dry after each coating. Normally the sugar is heated to the second degree.

To Make Brown Wafer

Take half a pint, of milk and half a pint of cream and put to it half a pound of brown sugar; melt and strain it through a sieve; take as much fine flour as will make one half of the milk and cream very stiff, then put in the other half; stir it all the while, that it may not be in lumps; then, put in two eggs well beaten, a little sack, some mace ground fine, two or three cloves beaten: bake in irons. (Borella)

NOTE: Use a light brown sugar. Sack is the name of white fortified wine imported from Spain. Today we can use white wine of our choice.

Baking in irons would mean a wafer iron. We can bake in a wafer or waffle maker.

To Make Tarts

Take apples, or pears, cut them in small quarters, and set them over the fire, with a piece of lemon peel, and some cinnamon; let them simmer in as much water as will cover them, till tender; and if you bake them in tin patty pans, butter them first, and lay over a thin paste; lay in some sugar, then the fruit, with three or four teaspoonfuls of the liquor they were simmered in; put in a little more sugar, and lid them over. If your tarts are made of apricots, green almonds, nectarines, or green plumbs, they must be scalded before you use them, and observe to put nothing to them but sugar, and as little water as possible; make use of the syrup they were scalded in, as you did for your apples, raspberries and all ripe fruit need not be scalded; and if you make your tarts in china or glass patties, lay the sugar at bottom, then the fruit with, a little more sugar on the top; no paste at the bottom, only lid them over, and bake them in a slack oven. You have receipts how: to make crusts for tarts; mince pies must be, baked in tin patties, that you may slip them out into a dish, and a puff paste is the best for them. When you make sweetmeat tarts, or a crocant tart, lay in the sweetmeats, or preserved fruits either in glass or china patties that are small for that purpose; lay a very thin crust on the top, and let them be baked no more than till your crust is nicely coloured, and that in a slow oven. If you would have a crocant tart for the middle of the table, or a side dish, have a glass, or china dish, of what use you please, and lay in the preserved served fruits of different sorts, (you must have a round cover just the size of the inside of your dish) roll out a sugar crust, the thickness of an Half crown, and lay over the cover; mark it with marking irons made on purpose for that use; of what shapes you please; then put the crust, with the cover, into a very slack oven, not to discolour it, only to have it crisp. When you take it out of the oven, loosen it from the cover very gently, and when quite cold, take it Carefully out and lay over your sweetmeats, and it being hollow, you will see the fruit through it. If the tart is not eaten, only take off the lid, and your sweetmeats may be put into the pots again. (Borella)

NOTE: Paste is pie crust. To "lid them over" is to cover with pie crust. You may also see in some receipts that it is a "coffin lid." A patty pan is a small tart pan or patty tin, and to butter them over is to grease the inside of the pan with butter, lard, or you can use shortening. Using anything other than butter will give it a different flavor. A sweetmeat is a delicacy made of preserved fruit with sugar. A crocant tart is made with a sugar crust, in this case not using vanilla which is traditionally used today. A half crown is 2.29mm or .09 inches — so very thin.

How to Keep Fruit for Tarts all the Year

Take your fruit when it is fit to pot, and strew some sugar at the bottom of the pot, then fruit, and then sugar; [and] so on till the pot is full; cover them with sugar, tie a bladder over the pot, then leather, and keep it in a dry place. (Glasse)

NOTE: This essentially layers fruit in sugar. A bladder in the time period would be from a sheep. There are fake bladders available commercially, or you could use plastic wrap and then leather to seal the lid (or buy pie filling).

To Make a Bread and Butter Puddings

Get a penny loaf and cut it into thin dices of bread and butter, as you do for tea. Butter your dish as you cut them, lay slices all over the dish, then strew a few currants clean washed and picked, then a row of bread and butter, then a few currants, and so on till all your bread and butter in; then take a pint of milk, beat up four eggs, a little salt, half a nutmeg grated, mix all together with sugar to your taste; pour this over the bread, and bake it half an hour. A puff-paste under does best. You may put in two spoonfuls of rose-water. (Glasse)

NOTE: Slice your bread about ¼ inch thick.

Tea Cream

PUT one ounce of the best tea in a pitcher, pour on it a table spoonful of water, and let it stand an hour to soften the leaves; then put to it a quart of boiling cream, cover it close, and in half an hour strain it; add four tea-spoonsful of a strong infusion of rennet in water, stir it, and set it on some hot ashes, and cover it; when you find by cooling a little of it, that it will jelly, pour it into glasses, and garnish with thin bits of preserved fruit. (Randolph)

NOTE: Rennet is the ingredient in which milk is coagulated to make cheese. There are different kinds of rennet. Today you can get a vegetable or microbial rennet versus the animal type they used in the time period.

Clouted Cream

TAKE four quarts of new milk from the cow and put it in a broad earthen pan, and let it stand till the next day, then put it over a very slow fire for half an hour; make it nearly hot to set the cream, then put it away till it is cold, and take the cream off, and beat it smooth with a spoon. It is accounted in the West of England very fine for tea or coffee, or to put over fruit tarts or pies. (Glasse)

NOTE: New milk from the cow is fresh. If you do not have access to fresh milk, use what you can get. Set it out to get close to room temperature, and then heat it for 30 minutes on low heat, and then increase it until you see the cream on the top, and set it aside to cool. There should be some cream on the top that you can skim off and then whip or wisk it to create the "clouted cream."

To Make Clotted Cream

Put one-Teaspoon of earning into a quart of good cream, when it comes to a curd break it very carefully with a silver spoon, lay it upon a sieve to drain a little, put it into a china soup plate, pour over it some good cream, with the kind of raspberries, damsons, or any kind of fruit to make it a pink colour, sweeten it to your taste, and lay round it a few strawberry leaves. — It is proper for a middle at supper, or a corner at dinner. (Raffald)

NOTE: Earning is runnet to turn milk into curds for making cheese. See the note for Tea Cream above. Damsons is a type of plum that is purple/black.

Baked Apples

TAKE a dozen fine, large juicy apples, and pare and core them, but do not cut them in pieces. Put them side by side into a large baking-pan, and fill up with white sugar the holes from whence you have extracted the cores. Pour into each a little lemon-juice, or a few drops of essence of lemon, and stick in every one a long piece of lemon-peel evenly cut. Into the bottom of the pan put a very little water, just enough to prevent the apples from burning. Bake them about an hour, or till they are tender all through, but not till they break. When done, set them away to get cold. If closely covered they will keep two days. They may be eaten at tea with cream. Or at dinner with a boiled custard poured over them. Or you may cover them with sweetened cream flavoured with a little essence of lemon, and whipped to a froth. Heap the froth over every apple so as to conceal them entirely. (Leslie)

NOTE: Essence of lemon is lemon peel soaked in vodka for 4-6 weeks. Essence in the time period is its scent or perfume.

Apple Butter

THIS is a compound of apples and cider boiled together till of the consistence of soft butter. It is a very good article on the tea-table, or at luncheon. It can only be made of sweet new cider fresh from the press, and not yet fermented. Fill a very large kettle with cider, and boil it till reduced to one half the original quantity. Then have ready some fine juicy apples, pared, cored, and quartered; and put as many into the kettle as can be kept moist by the cider. Stir it frequently, and when the apples are stewed quite soft, take them out with a skimmer that has holes in it, and put them into a tub. Then add more apples to the cider, and stew them soft in, the same manner, stirring them nearly all the time with a stick. Have at hand some more cider ready boiled, to thin the apple butter in case you should find it too thick in the kettle. If you make a large quantity, (and it is not worthwhile to prepare apple butter on a small scale,) it will take a day to stew the apples. At night leave them to cool in the tubs, (which must be covered with cloths,) and finish next day by boiling the apple and cider again till the consistence is that of soft marmalade, and the colour a very dark brown. Twenty minutes or half an hour before you finally take it from the fire, add powdered cinnamon, cloves, and nutmeg to your taste. If the spice is boiled too long, it will lose its flavour. When it is cold, put it into stone jars, and cover it closely. If it has been well made, and sufficiently boiled, it will keep a year or more. It must not be boiled in a brass or bell-metal kettle, on account of the verdigris which the acid will collect in it, and which will render the apple butter extremely unwholesome, not to say poisonous. (Leslie and Trula Mae Fisher)

NOTE: This recipe was shared with me from a friend's mother, and is similar to the way it was made in the time.

Isinglass Jelly

PUT an ounce of isinglass, and half an ounce of cloves, into a quart of water. Boil it to a pint, strain it upon a pound of loaf sugar, and when cold, sweeten your tea with it. You may add a little wine. Jellies made from calf's feet, and other things, have been already given. (Glasse)

NOTE: It is best just to use store purchased gelatin. This is included so you understand how it was made in the time. Isinglass is a "gelatin" taken from the swim bladders of fish, particularly sturgeon, and used to make jelly, glue, and clarifying ale.

To Colour Jellies

Your jellies made of hartshorn, or calves-feet or legs, may be made of what Colour you would have them. If white, use almonds pounded and strained after the usual manner; if yellow, put in some yolks of eggs; if red, some juice of red beet; if gray, a little cochineal; if purple, some purple turnsole or powder of violets; if green, some juice of beet leaves; which must be boiled in a dish to take away its crudity. (Nott)

NOTE: It is best just to use store purchased gelatin. This is included so you understand how it was made in the time.

The Way To Mould Ices In All Sorts Of Fruits

WHEN your composition is perfectly congealed, take a spoon and the moulds you want to make use of; fill these well with your ices as quickly and dexterously as you can: you must have besides just ready by you a bucket with pounded natural ice, and a great deal of salt; there you put your moulds in proportion as you fill them, and cover them directly with pounded ice and salt, continuing so doing to every mould you fill up till you have filled them all. When that is done you cover them quite and set them a full hour in that ice. When you want to take off what is in your moulds, you take a pan of water, and first wash well those moulds one after the other rub off all the salt which sticks round them, then you open your moulds put their contents in a china dish and send them up. You may give to every one of your ices the very colour of the fruit they represent; but then you must have your colour ready by you, and with a very fine pencil point them quickly, in which case they must likewise be served directly, or at least you must put them in the cave; then your cave must have been set in a bucket and prepared half an hour before you — take your fruits from the moulds: in that cave you are then to set them after they are coloured, till the moment come is of serving them, your fruit is certainly finer and takes the downy look of the natural one. (Borella)

NOTE: This receipt starts after you have made the ice cream or custard. A cave is the bucket of ice in which you keep the mould so it stays cold.

Receipts with or to Take with Tea

Directions For The Ices Made With Preserved Fruits

There are none of the ices which we have directed you how to make with fresh gathered fruit, but may be made also with that same sort of fruit after it has been preserved; in which case you are to proceed thus: Take your preserve of whatever sort it is, put it in a bason, mash it well and dissolve it as much as possible with a spoon, some lemon Juice and a little water to bring it to a pulp; pass it through a sieve: should they not be sweet enough add as much clarified sugar as is required, and when you have passed them through your sieve, put them in your sabotiere and make them congeal by working them as we directed before. (Borella)

NOTE: A sabotiere is a cylinder, normally copper, that is used to make ice cream. Goose Bay Workshops (www.goosebay-workshops.com) makes a lovely sabotiere for those interested in making it this way. Put your mixture into the sabotiere and the sabotiere goes inside a wooden bucket (which is your larger bason) that you then surround with ice. I then sprinkle an ice cream salt (bay salt) into the ice and let the sabotiere (now filled with the cream mixture) sit for about 10 minutes — and then I twist or spin it in the ice. I continue to do this for about 30-45 minutes of spinning, I open the "bason" and push contents down the sides and into the frozen part of the mixture. You will need a small wooden paddle or you can use a rubber kitchen scraper to push the cream down if not in a period appropriate environment. Check often your ice, refill it, and continue to sprinkle with salt. Continue this until the contents congeal or freeze. BE VERY CAREFUL with the water that sits in the bottom of the bucket — pour it on weeds that you want to kill as it is very toxic. DO NOT DRINK IT, PUT IT NEAR ANIMALS, ETC.

Tea Cream Ices

Make tea very strong in a tea-pot, have your cream ready mixt with the proper quantity of sugar and yolks of eggs, pass your cream through a sieve, pass likewise your tea over it, mix the whole well with a spoon, when that is done put it in the *sabotiere* and make it congeal according to the usual method. (Borella)

A Method to Make all Sorts of Light, Seed, and other Cakes

IT may not be improper to observe, that before you proceed to make any sort of cakes, that care should first be taken to have all your ingredients ready before you begin, then beat your eggs well, and not leave them till you have finished the cakes, for by such neglect, they would go back, and your cakes would not be light; if your cakes are to have butter in, take care you beat it to a fine cream before you put in your sugar, for if you beat it twice the time after it will not answer so well. (Borella)

NOTE: This is just instruction on how to proceed to make your cakes. Take heed and remember as you make them.

A White Currant Cake

TO two pounds of flour well dried, take a pound of sugar beat and sifted, one pound of butter, a quarter of an ounce of mace, the same of nutmegs, sixteen eggs, two pounds and a half of currants, picked and washed, half a pound of candied lemon, the same of sweet almonds, half a pint of sack or brandy, three spoonfulls of orange flower water, beat your butter to a cream, put in your sugar, beat the whites of your eggs half an hour, mix them with your sugar and butter, then beat your yolks half an hour, mix them with your whites, it will take two hours beating put in your flower a little before your oven is ready, mix your currants and all your other ingredients lightly in, just when you put it in your tin. Two hours will bake it. (Borella)

NOTE: Flower is flour. This receipt could be cut in half.

A Common Seed Cake

TAKE two pounds of flour, rub into it half a pound of powder sugar, one ounce of caraway seeds beaten, have ready a pint of milk, with half a pound of butter melted in it, and two spoonfuls of new barm, make it up into a paste, set it on the fire to rise, flour your tin, and bake it in a quick oven. (Borella)

NOTE: New barm is a type of yeast and you can use Brewer's Yeast in its place, and a quick oven is 425-450 degrees. Be sure to note the butter should already be melted in your milk.

To Make A Fine Saffron Cake
A Receipt practised by Mrs. Glass.
TAKE a quarter of a peck of fine flour, a pound and a half of fresh butter, a quarter of an ounce of mace and cinnamon together, beat fine, and mix the spice in the flour. Set on a quart of milk to boil, break the butter in, and stir it till the milk boils; take off all the butter, and a little of the milk; mix with the flour a pound of sugar beat fine, a penny-worth of saffron made into a tincture; take a pint of yeast that is not bitter, and stir it well into the remainder of the milk; beat up six eggs very well, and put to the yeast and milk, strain it to the flour, with some rose-water, and the tincture of saffron; beat up altogether with your hands lightly, and put it into a hoop or pan well Buttered. It will take an hour and an half in a quick oven. You may make the tincture of saffron with the rose water. (Borella)

NOTE: A tincture is "to impregnant with some quantity… or imbue with some tinct or colour." In this case "to take a penny-worth" is defined as "so much of any quantity as may be bought for a penny, a small quantity, an advantageous purchase." There is no way to identify what a "Penny's Worth" was — but I would use it sparingly. Less can be more in this case.

A Cake Rolled Up in the Form of a Snail
GET some puff paste and cream made after the same manner, as in the article of cream tarts or franchipane; you may make it either white or green. Spread your paste the length of one or two yards of the breadth of four or six fingers, and about the thickness of two crown pieces. Put your cream in the middle of the whole length of it, and close your paste so that your cream may not run out and make it in the shape of a large sausage.

This being done; put it on paper well buttered, turning it found to imitate the form of a snail, and rub it with beaten eggs. Bake it in a moderate oven and glaze it. (Borella)

NOTE: Franchipane is similar to marzipan — it is an almond-flavored cream or paste similar to a pastry cream. Marzipan is an almond paste. If you want to try to color it green, use concentrated spinach juice; for white use powdered almonds. Rolling it in to the shape of a snail would be fun! A crown piece was about 38mm or 1-½ inches in diameter. The thickness was about 3mm or just under ⅛ inch.

Chocolate Pastils

TAKE a little chocolate, which you put in a pan ever the fire to melt it, stir it with a spoon; when it is well melted, take half a pound of loaf sugar, pounded in a mortar and sifted, which you dissolve in a little clear water. When that is done, put in your chocolate, if you find the paste too thick add a little water, enough to bring it, to the that degree of liquidity we specified for the lemons; then dress it on half sheets of paper as we then directed, but do not put it in the stove for the heat softens chocolate; let it dry naturally in a cup-board, and when dry, take them off from the paper and put them in your boxes used for such kind of things. (Glasse)

NOTE: The degree used for lemons is in the second degree.

To Broil Salmon

CUT fresh salmon in thick pieces, flour them and broil them, lay them in your dish and have plain melted butter in a cup. (Glasse)

NOTE: This is another example of the receipt being written down and assuming the cook knows what to do. To broil means to "be in the heat." Broiled is "dressed by being laid on the coals, heated." Many modern ovens have a broiler in the bottom of the stove. This, when turned on, gets to 500-550 degrees Fahrenheit. It cooks your food very quickly, so take care not to burn the salmon. Once they are finished, you should melt some butter in which to either pour over or dip your pieces into. This does not call to season the salmon, so try it this way first, and then season to taste if making again. A tin or even cast iron pan would work well for this.

Salmon in Cases
CUT your salmon into little pieces, such as will lay rolled in half-sheets of paper. Season it with pepper salt, and nutmeg; butter the inside of the paper well, fold the paper so as nothing can come out, then lay them on a tin-plate to be baked, pour a little melted butter over the papers, and then crumbs of bread all over them. Do not let your oven be too hot, for fear of burning the paper. A tin oven before the fire does best. When you think they are enough, serve them up just as they are. There will be sauce enough in the papers. (Glasse)

NOTE: Use baking paper. A tin oven is a baking oven that you set before the fire and the light reflects off the back to help bake it. If making this in an oven at home, you can use baking paper on a baking sheet. I have tied the paper closed so it does not leak with a butcher's twine or baking string.

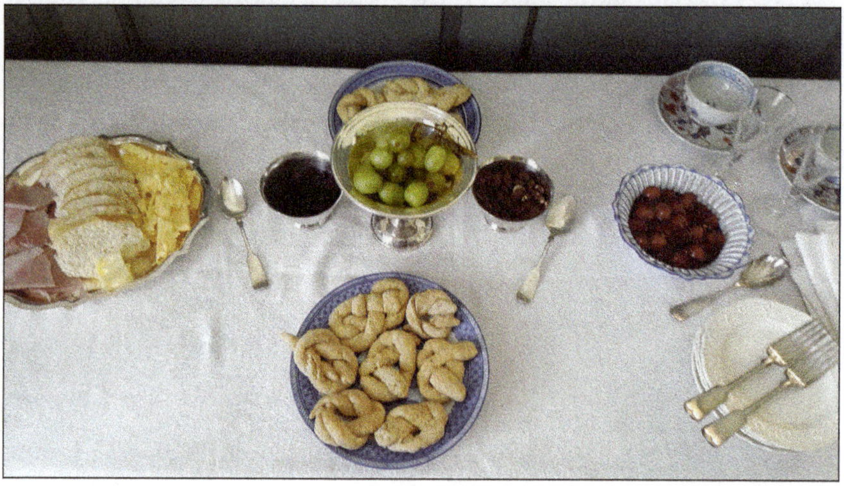

CHAPTER 7

Dessert Bills Of Fare.

Hannah Glasse says in her confectionary book that, "Families have desired I would in my Book of Cookery give them a few bills of fare of little desserts, fit for private families; but as it is a thing depends entirely on fancy, and indeed, what they have to set it out with, and the seasons of the year for fruits, &tc., I am at some loss how give to directions in writing; but as it may be a little guide to the young and unexperienced, I have given them in the best manner I can, agreeable to the method they are now set out; ice cream is a thing used in fall desserts, as it is to be had both winter and summer, and what in London is always to be had at the confectioners."

She continues by saying "Giving directions for a grand dessert would be needless, for those persons who give such grand desserts, either keep a proper person, or have them of a confectioner, who not only has everything wanted, but every ornament to adorn it with, without giving any trouble to the family, when supposed to be taken up with other affairs ; though — every young lady out to know both how to make all kinds of confectionary and dress out a desert; in former days, it was locked, on as a great perfection of a lady to understand all these things, if it was only to give directions to her servants; and our dames of old, did not think it any disgrace to understand cookery and confectionary. But for country ladies, it is a pretty amusement, both to make the sweetmeats and dress out a dessert, as it depends wholly on fancy and but little expense." (Glasse)

The following are Bills of Fare for Small "Deserts" from Borella, Glasse, and Nott show a multitude of dishes as they would be set on a table during dessert or also possibly for taking tea.

During the time period, fruits, vegetables, and meats were available by season and also served during tea. Within *A Book of Cookery by A Lady*, you can find seasonable items by month, so when making one of these dessert collations, be cognizant or mixing and matching dishes with when foods were in season.

These bills of fare show a center piece, but while taking tea, your tea pot could be the center piece and the water urn, if you have one, set on a separate table. There was really no true specific way in which to do this. The amount of dishes on the table would reflect how many you would be serving. These are possibly representative of a third course of a meal as well. Often times the tea table was just that — for tea — and a sideboard would hold all of the other dishes.

Additionally, many of these items are available in our grocery stores today, but I have found that making the receipts as they were in the 18th century gives us a better idea of the tastes they had, although we will never truly know. I believe that the fruits, vegetables, and meats of today taste differently than they did then because of the changes in agriculture and animal husbandry.

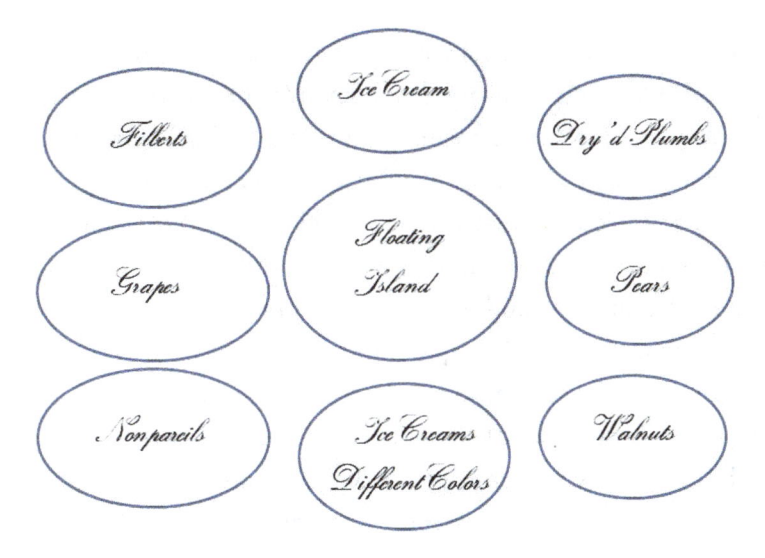

Dessert Bills Of Fare

- Filberts
- Ice Cream
- Dry'd Plumbs
- Grapes
- Floating Island
- Pears
- Nonpareils
- Ice Creams Different Colors
- Walnuts

Ice Cream

Take two pewter basons, one larger than the other; the inward one must have a close cover, into which you put your cream, and mix it with what you think proper, to give it a flavour and colour, as raspberries, &c. then sweeten it to your palate, cover it close, and set it in the larger bason ; fill it with ice, and a large handful of salt under and over and round about ; let it stand in the ice three quarters of an hour, uncover, and stir it and the cream well together, then cover it again ; let it stand half an hour longer, and turn it into your plate ; your basons should be three cornered, that four colours may lie in one plate ; one colour should be yellow, another green, another red, and a fourth white; but that depends on fancy, and what you colour them with ; as any fort of fruit, saffron, or cochineal; and for the green, there are several forts of juice; all must be well flavoured with different sorts of fruit; the white wants nothing but orange-flower water and sugar, three basons are made at the pewterers for the use above. Some make their ice cream in tin pans, and mix three pennyworth of salt petre and two pennyworth of roach allum, both beat fine, with the ice, as also three pennyworth of bay salt ; lay it round the pan as above, cover it with a coarse cloth, and let it stand two hours. (Glasse)

115

NOTE: This receipt tells you how to make ice cream. Get a heavy cream and sweeten it with sugar and flavor/color it with a fruit of your choice. You can then put the cream mixture into a small bason. I have used a copper sabotiere inside a wooden bucket (which is your larger bason) that you then surround with ice. I then sprinkle an ice cream salt (bay salt) into the ice and let the sabotiere (now filled with the cream mixture) sit for about 10 minutes — and then I twist or spin it in the ice. I continue to do this for about 30–45 minutes of spinning, I open the "bason" and push the cream down the sides and into the frozen part of the cream. You will need a small wooden paddle or you can use a rubber kitchen scraper to push the cream down if not in a period appropriate environment. Check often your ice, refill it, and continue to sprinkle with salt. Continue this until all of your cream is frozen. BE VERY CAREFUL with the water that sits in the bottom of the bucket — pour it on weeds that you want to kill as it is very toxic. DO NOT DRINK IT, PUT IT NEAR ANIMALS, ETC. Another way that this describes is to put your cream mixture into a pan and lay it down into the ice/salt (salt petre/roach allum) pan for two hours covered or just put it in your freezer in a pan.

Of Strawberries and Iced Creams

MAKE an almond paste, as before directed put it in a baking dish, and raise a border as to any other sorts of paste; it requires but a short time to bake, and very little heat; just before you are ready to serve, put ice cream in it not very hard, and the strawberries upon it; this ice cream is made with a pint of good cream, and sugar sufficient to make it pretty sweet, a little orange flower water, two yolks of eggs; put it on the fire till it is ready to boil, stir it, to mix the eggs very well; when it is cold, put it in a mould to ice, as is explained in ice cream articles; you may also boil pistachio nuts in this cream, and sift it before icing. (Borella)

NOTE: Marzipan is an almond paste. It can be purchased or made. It is essentially ground almonds, confectioner's sugar, extract flavoring, and salt. *The Cooks and Confectioners Dictionary: Or, The Accomplish'd*

Housewives by John Nott also has Almond Butter, Almond Cheese, Almond Cakes, etc., and other almond receipts that look yummy.

To keep Wallnuts, or Filberds, all the year

Gather them when they are ripe, with the green husks on, bury them in dry sand, and mix the filberts with them. (Glasse)

NOTE: A filberd is a hazelnut. This essentially tells you how they were able to keep and preserve walnuts and hazelnuts so they could have them available longer so they did not spoil.

To keep Grapes, Gooseberries, Apricots, Peaches, Nectarines, Cherries, Currants, and Plumbs, the Whole Year

Take fine dry sand, that has little or no saltness in it, and make it as dry as possible with often turning it in the sun; gather your fruits when they are just ripening, or coming near ripe, and dip the ends of the stalks in melted pitch or bees wax; and having a large box with a close lid, dry your fruit a little in the sun to take away the superfluous moisture, and lightly spread a layer of sand at the bottom of the box, and a layer of fruit on it, but not too near each other; then scatter sand very even about an inch thick over them, and so another layer till the box is full; then shut the lid down close, that the air may not penetrate; and whenever you take out anything, be sure to mind the placing them even again; so you will have them fit for tarts, or other uses, till the next season; if they are a little wrinkled, wash them in warm water and they will plump up again: you may use millet instead of sand if you think it more convenient. (Glasse)

NOTE: This essentially tells you how they were able to keep and preserve these fruits so they could have them available longer so they did not spoil. Millet is a plant that has small seeds that are used to make flour.

The Floating Island

Take a quart of very thick cream, sweeten it with fine sugar, grate in the peel of two lemons, and half a pint of sweet white wine; then whisk it well, till you have railed all the froth you can, pour a pint or quart of thick cream into a china dish, according to the depth of your dish; take two French rolls, slice them thin, and lay them over the cream as light as you can; then a layer of fine clear calves-foot jelly, or hartshorn jelly; then roll them over the currant jelly, then put the French rolls, and whip up your cream, lay it on as high as you can, and what remains pour into the bottom of the dish; garnish the rim of your dish with different sorts of sweetmeats, jellies, and ratafia cakes; this looks very ornamental in the middle of the table. (Glasse)

NOTE: This looks to be a complicated dish, but really isn't. The first part is a frothed lemon cream that you put into a deep dish. You take some bread and slice them thin. Then you add a layer of your choice of jelly and then on top of that use a currant jelly. Layer it as high as you want, and decorate/surround with sweatmeats, ratafia cakes, and other jellies. A ratafia cake is a small macaroon or an almond flavored cookie. You can use what you have or want to surround the contents of this dish. Hartshorn are deer antlers, and they are boiled to a liquid form and cooled. The cooled liquid forms into a gelatinous mass. I'd suggest using gelatin or Jello brand gelatin available in your grocery store.

To Stew Pears Purple

PARE four pears, cut them into quarters, core them, put them into a stew-pan, with a quarter of a pint of water, a quarter of a pound of sugar, cover them with a pewter-plate, then cover the pan with the lid, and do them over a slow fire. Look at them often, for fear of melting the plate; when they are: enough, and the liquor looks of a fine purple, take them off, and lay them in your dish with the liquor; when cold, serve them up for a side-dish at a second course, or just as you please. (Glasse)

NOTE: I have made these without the pewter plate. I cover them with the lid of my pan. Cook them very slow and not too done or they will fall apart. They are wonderful.

Dessert Bills Of Fare

Nonpareils

Nonpareils may be reckoned among the first species of confectionary, and from their great utility, will last, probably, as long as the art itself. Put into the pan over the barrel half a pound of Florence orris-root, pulverized and sifted, and warmed with a gentle fire. Take about half a table spoonful of syrup boiled to a pearl, moisten the powder with it, and with your hands make them into small grains; increase the charges by degrees, sift the nonpareils to take off the small particles and dust of the sugar; repeat the sifting often, taking care to have sieves of different sizes. At night place the nonpareils in the stove to dry, increasing them in size day after day with the finest sugar, and finish as above. Half a pound of orris will make more than a hundred weight of nonpareils. (Jarrin)

NOTE: Orris root is the root of the Iris plant. You can buy it in a powdered form in which to make this, but there are some cautions when using it. It seems to be safe with no known side effects; however, caution must be taken if you are pregnant and/or breast-feeding. When in doubt, buy the candy sprinkles in the baking aisle of the store.

To Colour Nonpareils

Prepare your colours, and take syrup boiled to a thread; mix your colours in separate pots, and divide the nonpareils; the quantity of white nonpareils being double that of any other colour, this being necessary to set off the other colours to advantage. Put one of the portions of your nonpareils into a pan, warm them, and pour on your colour; stir them well till they are all separated, and put them into the stove to dry. It is very important to give the exact quantity of colour, that the surface only of the nonpareils may be wet, and to leave them in the stove only time enough to dry them, as too much heat will make the colours fade. (Jarrin)

NOTE: See Chapter 11 — Colours of Confectionary section. See Nonpareils receipt above.

To Preserve Walnuts White

Take the largest French walnuts, when full grown; but before they are hard, pare off the green shell to the white, put them into fair water, and boil them till very tender; drain them and put them into clarified sugar, giving them a gentle heat; the next day boil some more sugar to blow, put it to them and give them a boil; the next day boil some more sugar to blow very strong, put it to the walnuts, give them a boil, scum: them and put them by; then drain them and put them on plates; dust them and put them into a warm stove to dry. (Glasse)

NOTE: These are essentially a candied or sugar glazed walnut dusted with sugar.

To Keep Walnuts All The Year Moist

Gather your nuts in a very dry day, and take care they don't lay on the ground to be bruised; as you gather them, put them into a deep earthen pot, when full, cover them with a paper, and then with a leather, and over that a wet bladder; set them in a dry place. (Glasse)

NOTE: A wet bladder is a sheep's bladder. There are faux sheep's bladders that can be purchased today, just use paper, or buy walnuts when you need them.

Dessert Bills Of Fare

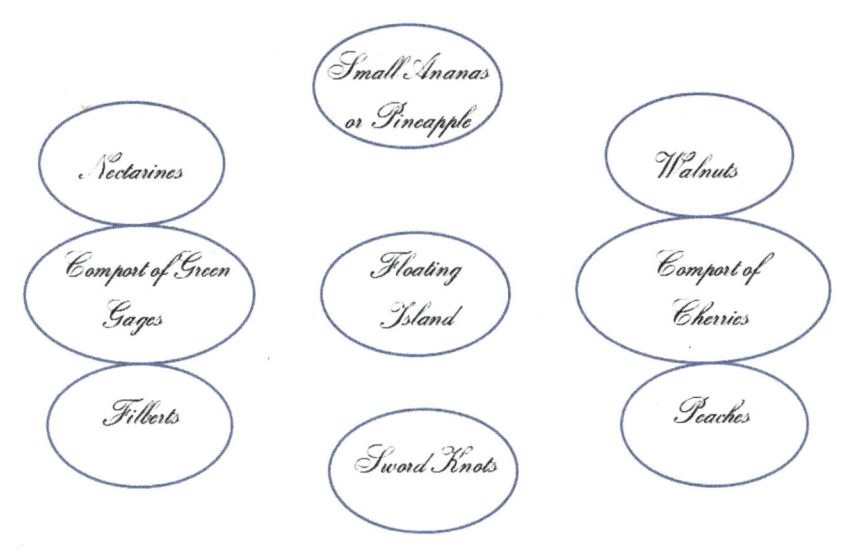

- Small Ananas or Pineapple
- Nectarines
- Walnuts
- Comport of Green Gages
- Floating Island
- Comport of Cherries
- Filberts
- Peaches
- Sword Knots

NOTE: Filberts are also known as Hazelnuts. Green Gages are a type of plumb. These dishes could be made starting in about June when cherries, apricots, and plumbs are in season if you want to use fresh fruit.

Moist Ananas Or Pine Apples

TAKE any quantity of ananas, cut them into four quarters, or in round slices, and pare off the skin, then take clarified sugar and water, in equal quantities, put in the ananas and do them as the other above-mentioned fruits, taking care to skim them well during the time you are doing them for it is very essential to remark, that when you are making any sort of preserves whatever, if you do not skim them well they are apt to grow sour, which occasions a great deal of trouble to repair them again. You must not boil the ananas in water first, as we have directed for the other fruits, because it would deprive it of its best substance and flavour.

NOTE: To do them as the above-mentioned fruits are to, "put a pan of water on the fire, and when it boils put your pineapple in it, and boil them in, with a slow fire, till they become a little soft then take them off the fire, and throw them immediately in another pan of fresh water; have again another pan of fresh water…then take a preserving pan, put in it some of the first degree of your clarified sugar, put your pineapple in it, and let them boil about twelve minutes, taking care to take off all the scum they will throw; then take them out from the fire and put them in an earthen vessel; you will repeat this operation during four days running, and strain the sugar off every time, and boil it before you put the pineapple in, because, as you will perceive, the sugar always throws off a white scum, which must be taken off; and it is after that, you must put your pineapple in and boil them, as I said. When you see the syrup is very thick, and that your pineapple have well taken the sugar, put them in pots, and take care they should be well covered with syrup, or else they will soon turn mouldy. Cover them with paper or parchment." Off of the "fire" is also off of the stove if making this at home.

Green Gages
Take any quantity of green gages prick them with a pin, put them in a pan with water, and set them on the fire; when you see the water is beginning to boil, take them off and leave them in that same water to cool till the next day. When you are to set them again on a very gentle fire, that they may turn green When you see they are green enough, you put them in a sieve to drain; then you take the first degree of clarified sugar, in which you add three parts water, then the plumbs, and set the whole on a slow fire to make them throw off their water; Sifter which, you put them in a pan for two days, and then you add clarified sugar, and proceed as for the above preserves. (Borella)

NOTE: Green Gages are a type of plumb. See the "Moist Ananas Or Pine Apples" receipt to proceed as for the preserves.

A Floating Island
TAKE a quart of thick cream, a gill of sack, the rind of lemon grated, sweeten it to your taste, mill it till it is of a thick froth & then carefully pour the thin from the froth into a deep dish, cut then some french roll, lay a slice as light as possible on the cream, then a layer of currant jelly on that, then another thin slice of roll, then hartshorn jelly, then roll; and

over that whip the froth which you save off the cream very well and lay at top as high as you can. Garnish the rim of the dish with sweetmeats and flowers: it looks well for a middle dish by candle light. (Borella)

NOTE: See the floating island in the first dessert collation as well by Hannah Glasse.

Compotes of Cherries

Take cherries, and cut off half of their stalks; have clarified sugar, put your cherries –in your pot let them boil till you see they are done enough; then take them off soon the fire, and them stand till they are grown cold enough to take them all one by one, and set them on their stalk upwards in your china dishes; and pour dishes. If you see your sugar is in jelly, you must put them directly in your china dishes and pour your sugar over them. (Borella)

NOTE: These call for you to keep the cherries stalks (or stem) on the cherries you purchase and sugar them in clarified sugar.

Moist Peaches

TAKE any quantity of peaches, rub well all their down with a cloth, and prick them with a large pin as much as you please. Have a pan of water on the fire, in which you put your peaches, and do them thus with a slow fire taking a great care they should not boil, for you would run the risk, of their bursting. When you perceive they are a little softened, take them off, and put them into fresh water; after which, you do for sugar just the same as we have said about the pears.

NOTE: Borella also notes for pears that you can preserve them in the proper method of the time. If you are to serve them right away, then just sugar them and serve. If you are to present you are to do the following: "have again another pan of fresh water, in which you squeeze three lemons, pare your pears and put them in that lemon water: they will turn as white as snow; then take a preserving pan, put in it some of the first degree of your clarified sugar, put your pears in it, and let them boil about twelve minutes, taking care to take off all the scum they will throw; then take them out from the fire and put them in an earthen vessel; you will repeat this operation during four days running, and strain the sugar off every time, and boil it before you put the pears in, because, as you will perceive, the sugar always throws off a white scum, which must be taken off; and it is after that, you must put your pears in and boil them, as I said. When you see the syrup is very thick, and that your pears have well taken the sugar, put them in pots, and take care they should be well covered with syrup, or else they will soon turn mouldy. Cover them with paper or parchment.

Sword Knots

MAKE a second-best paste and roll it very thin; cut it in thongs like ribbons, some with a knife, and some with a dented paste cutter, to make the scollop; fold them like a sword knot; wet the paste with eggs, where it should join together; bake them on a baking plate; and when ready to serve, garnish with currant jelly, apricot marmalade, frothed cream, or anything else. (Borella)

NOTE: This receipt does not tell you what the "second-best paste" is. However, Borella does note several types of paste to make — one of them is called "Royal Paste" and is written below. I have also included "A Puff Paste for Tarts or Pyes with Fruit, Preserves, and Other Sweet Meats." You can also fold these like pretzels or other shapes as well.

Royal Paste

BOIL a pint of water a moment, with a little sugar, a quarter of a pound of butter, a little fine or rasped lemon peel, a little salt, put flour to it, by little and little, to mix it well, and pretty thick; turn and stir it continually on the fire, until it quits the pan; take it off, and while it is warm, put eggs to it, one by one, mix it well, and put eggs, until it is come to the consistency of a paste, and sticks to the fingers. (Borella)

NOTE: This is a type of pie crust that can be used for tarts, pies, etc. The receipt does not call for measurement of the water, sugar, butter, lemon peel, salt, flour or the amount of eggs! The rule of thumb for pastry is two to one.

A Puff Paste for Tarts or Pyes with Fruit, Preserves, and Other Sweet Meats

TAKE two handfuls of fine flour, put it on a clean table, make a hollow in the middle of your flour, put in an egg, with a bit of butter the bigness of an egg, and a little salt, if the butter is fresh. Wet the flour with cold water, let your paste be as stiff as your butter, then roll it, spread it over with butter, double the paste, it once or twice or more, till the butter is well mixed in the paste. Rowl it for an under-crust, put it in a baking-pan, then put in a marmalade either of preserved apples, cherries, apricots, gooseberries, jelly, or any other sort; now roll your paste very thin, flour it, double it four or five times, then cut it into long and thin slices, place them on the top of your tarts in what shape you think fit; put round it a slip of the same paste, of about the breadth of a thumb, which slip pare off neatly. Your tart being done either in the oven or in a baking-pan with fire under and over, straw some sugar over it, glaze it with a red-hot fire-shovel, then dish it up, and serve it either hot or cold. (Borella)

NOTE: Wonderful puff paste. They describe the expected consistency of the paste as fresh cold butter. "Rowl" is roll. Straw is strew or sprinkle sugar over it. Also glaze it by using a salamander.

Sugar Pears — Bloomage — Nuts

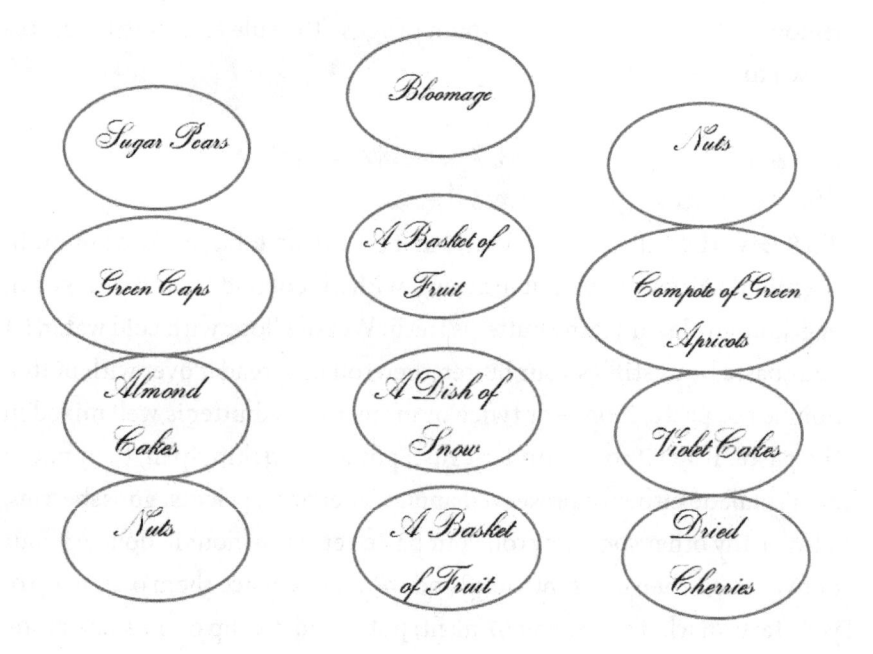

Green Caps — A Basket of Fruit — Compote of Green Apricots

Almond Cakes — A Dish of Snow — Violet Cakes

Nuts — A Basket of Fruit — Dried Cherries

Bloomage

Take clear hartshorn or calves-foot jelly, make it pretty sweet, put in a little orange flower water, a little rose water, a little wine, and the juice of an orange ; put in as much of all the ingredients as will make it palatable, blanch some sweet almonds and pound them in a mortar with the orange flower and rose water, as much as will turn the bloomage white, and strain it well; stir all together till you find it jelly, which you will know by taking a little out in a spoon; pour it what thing you please to shape it in, and when cold turn it out and stick it with almonds ; if it sticks, dip your bason or glasses in hot water. (Glasse, 1765)

NOTE: Hartshorn are deer antlers, calves-foot is the hooves of calves. They are boiled to a liquid form and cooled. The cooled liquid forms into a gelatinous mass. Bloomage is essentially your 18th century gelatin with flavoring and almonds in it. I'd suggest using gelatin or Jello brand gelatin available in your grocery store.

Sugar Pears

Take any quantity of pears, which should be but half ripe, make a split on their head cross ways with a knife, no deeper than the heart. After this is done, put a pan of water on the fire, and when it boils put your pears in it, and boil them in, with a slow fire, till they become a little soft ; then take them off the fire, and throw them immediately in another pan of fresh water; have again another pan of fresh water, in which you squeeze three lemons, pare your pears and put them in that lemon water: they will turn as white as snow; then take a preserving pan, put in it some of the first degree of your clarified sugar, put your pears in it, and let them boil about twelve minutes, taking care to take off all the scum they will throw; then take them out from the fire and put them in: an earthen vessel; you will repeat this operation during four days running, and strain the sugar off every time, and boil it before you put the pears in, because, as you will perceive, the sugar always throws off a white scum, which must be taken off; and it is after that, you must put your pears in and boil them, as I said. When you see the syrup is very thick, and that your pears have well taken the sugar, put them in pots, and take care they should be well covered with syrup, or else they will soon turn mouldy. Cover them with paper or parchment. (Borella)

NOTE: This does not have specific measurements or numbers, so it allows you to get creative! The very first sentence essentially tells you to cut the pear down halfway, but not all the way through. It does not tell you to peel them, so try it with peel and without to see how they do. The "scum" is the sugar froth that comes up to the top of the water when boiling — just skim it off. You can make this and have them ready to eat, or you can make them and put them in an earthen pot as mentioned so that the pears absorb the sugar over days. The syrup of the pears is what you could cover them with so they keep. You can buy a cooking parchment paper at the grocery store.

To Make Green Caps

TAKE codlings just before they are ripe, green them as for preserving, then rub them over with a little oiled butter and grate double refined sugar over them and set them in the oven till they look bright and sparkle like frost; then put them in a dish, and stick single flowers in every apple; pour round a fine custard it is a corner dish for dinner or supper. (Borella)

NOTE: A codling is a green cooking apple. Green caps are apples. See a Book of Cookery by a Lady for a lovely fine custard receipt. I do not think that "oiled butter" means having oil in butter. This could mean two things, either clarified butter or butter with extra fat in it. To clarify butter, you boil butter and try to get as much of the water to boil out of it. You boil it down, and then strain it through cheesecloth or a filter to get any particles out of it.

To Make Black Caps

TAKE six large apples, cut a slice off the top, put them in a tin and set them in a quick oven till they are brown, then with rose water wet them; grate a little sugar over them, set them in the oven again till they look bright and very black; then put them in a china dish and pour round them thick cream custard. (Borella)

NOTE: This is self explanatory. You can find a great cream custard receipt in *A Book of Cookery by a Lady* or use one you purchase.

A Dish of Snow

PUT in cold water twelve large apples them on a slow fire, when soft put them on a hair sieve, skin them, put the pulp in a bason, beat the whites of twelve eggs into a froth; sift half a pound of double refined sugar, and strew it in the eggs; beat the pulp of your apples to a froth, and beat them altogether till they are like a stiff snow; lay it on a china dish heaped as high as you can, and set round green knots of paste in imitation of Chinese rails, stick a sprig of myrtle in the dish and serve it up. (Borella)

Dessert Bills Of Fare.

NOTE: You should bake, ahead of time, pie dough or paste colored green, made into fence railing (railing meant "enclosing with rails" with rails meaning "to range in a line." The "Chinese rail" at the time can be seen in the book by Thomas Chippendale called, *The gentleman and cabinet-maker's director: being a large collection of the most elegant and useful designs of household furniture in the Gothic, Chinese and modern taste*, 1754 (drawing below). There were many styles that we can point to that were very intricate in design. A wonderful example is shown in the Paca House and Gardens in Annapolis, Maryland upstairs railings.

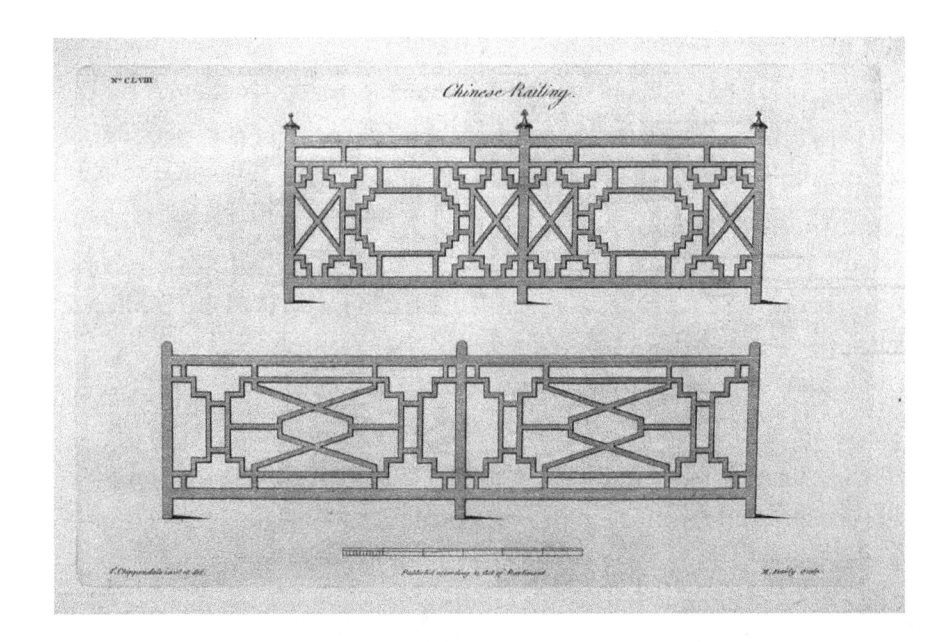

After you skin the apples and cook them, take the inside (pulp) and put it in a dish (bason). You should then put the pulp in a strainer (hair sieve) to drain them well. You would then take the white of the eggs and wisk them into a froth. After you sift the sugar, you strew it into the eggs. Then you do the same with your apples, and then put altogether into the egg/sugar froth, and beat them altogether until they are stiff and put into your decorative dish inside the Chinese railings. It does not state that you cook the mixture, so experiment with it.

Almond Cakes

TAKE a pound of double refined sugar finely seered, a quarter of a pound of the best almonds laid in cold water all night and blanched; take the white of an egg, put to it a spoonful of rose-water, and beat it to the whiteness of snow, letting it stand half an hour; beat your almonds, putting thereto a spoonful of rose-water, a little at once, and the same with the egg; when the almonds are well beat, put the sugar in by degrees, and minding you wet not the paste too much whilst you roll out the cakes; you must continue beating till all be used, and when your cakes are made, lay them severally on papers with some sifted sugar over them; bake them in an oven as hot as for your sugar cakes. (Borella)

NOTE: Seered means "dry or withered" in the time, today "seared" means to scorch or burn. This receipt tell you to bake them as hot as your "sugar cakes." Sugar cakes are sugar cookies and are baked in a moderate oven (or 350-400 degrees).

To Make Lemon, Orange, And Flower Cakes

TAKE sugar finely seered, and wet it with the juice of orange, or any flowers you fancy; there must be no more juice than will make your paste stiff and thick; set it upon the fire, when it begins to boil drop it in little cakes, and they will come off presently; scurvigrass done thus is good against the scurvy; if it boils you will spoil it. (Borella)

NOTE: This is an interesting receipt in that it tells you to take dry sugar and the juice of orange (or any flower which is your flavoring) but not how much to make a stiff paste or cookie dough. Start out with less juice and increase it until you get the consistency of paste. Then you are to put it on the fire or heat, and get it hot enough, and when it begins to boil, you put in little cakes but it doesn't tell you what cakes? This sounds almost like dumplings that will form into "cakes" once dropped into the water. I would make up the "paste" from the Royal Paste or Puff Paste receipt above, form them into balls or small shapes, and drop it into the water. We now know that citrus juices have vitamin C which is needed to prevent scurvy. Scurvigrass is a plant that used to be eaten by sailors to prevent scurvy as well. Do not leave them in longer as it can over cook them "or spoil it."

Violet Cakes
BEAT your sugar wherein gum hath been steeped, put in the violets and the juice, and so work it well together with seered sugar, and dry them in a stove. (Borella)

NOTE: To understand what this receipt is all about, we need to add another on "Gum Cakes" to know what "gum" is. I believe these are a candy using sugar and juice from violets. Today we can get Violet simple syrup as a substitute, and Gum-Tex used in making candies today instead of "gum."

To make Gum Cakes
TAKE gum tragacanth, commonly called gum dragon, let it lie all night in rose water till it is dissolved, have double-refined sugar beaten and seered, and mix your gum and sugar together; make it up into paste, then roll some up plain, and some with herbs and flowers; all the paste must be kept separately our herbs and flowers must be beat small before you make them into paste; but you may use the juice of the flowers and herbs only; I use sweet marjoram, red roses, clove-gilly-flowers, and blue-bottle berries, all clipped from the white again, for two colours will not do well; so roll them up, and cut them the bigness of a sixpence, but in what fashion you please, minding that they are rolled very thin. (Borella)

NOTE: Today we can get "Gum-Tex" or another agent used in making candies instead of "gum tragacanth" or "gum dragon." Then flavor it with rose-water, cloves, marjoram, blueberries, etc.

Dry Cherries In Bunches

TAKE Kentilh or morella cherries, and tye them in bunches with a thread, about a dozen a bunch and when you have dried your cherries, put the syrup that comes out of them to your bunches; let them just boil, cover them close, the next day scald them; and when they are close, lay them in sieves in a cool oven; turn them, and heat the oven every day till they are dry. (Borella)

NOTE: This essentially is dried cherries. You can follow this receipt by tying up some cherries and any juice that comes from them into a pot and then you put the cherries in the juice and boil them. Let them sit overnight and then scald them and when they are done, cool them, heat them again, until they are dry. You can also just purchase dried cherries!

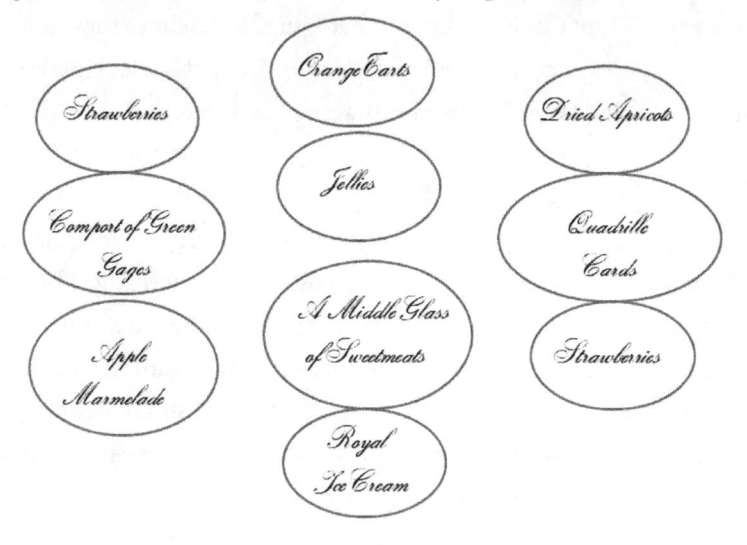

- Strawberries
- Orange Tarts
- Dried Apricots
- Comport of Green Gages
- Jellies
- Quadrille Cards
- Apple Marmelade
- A Middle Glass of Sweetmeats
- Strawberries
- Royal Ice Cream

Orange or Lemon Tart

TAKE six large lemons, and rub them very well with salt, and put them in water for two days, with a handful of salt in it; then change them into fresh water every day, (without salt) for a fortnight, then boil them two or three hours till they are tender, then cut them into half quarters, and then cut them three corner ways, as thin as you can: take six pippins pared, cored,

Dessert Bills Of Fare

and quartered, and a pint of fair water. Let them boil till the pippins break; put the liquor to your orange or lemon, and half the pippins well broken, and a pound of sugar. Boil these together a quarter of an hour, then put it in a gallipot, and squeeze an orange in it; if it be a lemon tart, squeeze a lemon; two spoonfuls is enough for a tart. Your patty pans must be small and shallow. Put fine puff paste, and very thin; a little while will bake it. Just as your tarts are going into the oven, with a feather, or brush them over with melted butter, and then sift double refined sugar over them; and this is a pretty icing on them. (Borella)

NOTE: Try this receipt as mentioned, it seems they are taking the acid out of the lemons and then adding them to the apples in water. A fortnight is 2 weeks. A gallipot is a small earthenware pot often used in apothecaries. Patty pans are small tart pans.

Whole Strawberries

TAKE any quantity of strawberries, pick off their stalks, and wash them well in cold water, and drain them; take clarified sugar of the ninth degree and let them Cool; When it is cold, put your strawberries in and set the whole again upon the fire, till they begin to feel the heat, take them off quickly and put them in a pan till the next day, when you put: them again on the fire and boil them very gently, for fear they should mash; when the syrup is a little thickened take them off and pot them. (Borella)

NOTE: How to clarify sugar and what the ninth degree means is in the cooking terms section. This essentially candies strawberries.

Directions for making of Fruit Jellies

IT is necessary to observe, that as these jellies are directed to be done much in the same manner as the marmalades; that a material difference must be observed in sifting the different sorts of fruits, not to force anything but the juices, which make the jellies clearer, and ought, for that purpose, to be strained in linen cloth. (Borella)

NOTE: This essentially is telling you how to take fruit and make it into juice to flavor your jellies. You can use any fruit and boil it down to a thick consistency. Check out the **Marmalade of Apples or Pears** below for more details.

To Make Fine Syllabubs

TAKE a pint of Rheinish, half a pint of sack squeeze in the juice of three lemons, take five half pints of cream, sweeten it with double, refined sugar, put all together whisk it half an hour; take it with a spoon fill the glasses with it, is best a day or two old, but cold weather they will be good a week or more days. (Borella)

NOTE: Rheinish is a white wine, sack is sherry. Sweeten to taste.

Light Light Whipt Syllabubs

TO a quart of thick cream put the juice of two Seville oranges, grate the peel of two lemons, put half a pound of double refined sugar pounded half a pint of sack, put a little red wine and sugar into the bottom of the glasses, some a little sack, and some a little syllabub; then whisk your syllabub up, take off the froth and fill the glasses carefully. They must not be made long before they are used. (Borella)

NOTE: This calls to drink it as soon as possible.

To Make A Hartshorn Flummery

Boil half a pound of the shavings of hartshorn in three pints of water till it comes to a pint, then strain it through a sieve into a bason, and set it by to cool then set it over the fire, let it just melt, and put to it half a pint of thick cream, scalded and grown cold again, a quarter of a pint of white wine, and two spoonfuls of orange-flour water and sweeten it with sugar, and beat it for an hour and a half, or it will not mix well, nor look well; dip your cups in water before you put in the flummery, or else it will not turn out well. It is best when it stands a day or two before you turn it out. When you serve it up, turn it out of the cups, and stick blanched almonds cut in long narrow bits on the top. You may eat them either with wine or cream. (Glasse)

NOTE: This is easily done with gelatin purchased from the store and then use white wine, orange flower water, and sugar to flavor it. Either cut almonds or purchase them already cut in which to stick into the top to decorate.

To Make Quadrille Cards

TAKE six square tins the size of a card fill them with very stiff flummery, when you turn them out, have ready a little cochineal dissolved in brandy, strain it through a muslin rag then take a camel's hair pencil, and make hearts and diamonds; for spades and clubs, take a little chocolate with a little sweet oil upon a marble, rub it till it is fine and bright, if you chuse the suit to be in hearts, you must place the ace of spades first, then the seven of hearts, then the ace of clubs, then the ace of hearts, then the two and three of hearts: if in diamonds the same as hearts, but if you chuse the suit in black then place the ace of spades, the two of spades, and the ace of clubs, the three, four and five of spades. Do the same in clubs: observe that the two black aces are always trumps in any suit. Pour a little Lisbon wine into the dish and send it up. (Borella)

NOTE: A flummery is a creamy confection or pudding baked with or on oatmeal, barley, rice flour, or wheat bran. Cochineal is a beetle and can be found to color the cards red. A "camel hair pencil" is a paint brush that you use to paint the shapes onto the flummery. A bit of liquid chocolate will allow you to make another suit, and so on. Lisbon wine is a red wine

Marmalade of Apples or Pears

PEEL and cut any quantity of golden pippins in thin slices, boil them with a little water very tender, pass them through a fine hair sieve and put the marmalade on the fire to reduce the liquid part; then put it to as much weight of the ninth degree of clarified sugar on a slow fire, to simmer a little while, stirring it continually, to mix them both well together, then put it in pots for use, observing to let it be cold before you cover it, proceed for doing the pears in the same manner. (Borella)

NOTE: So you can do this the hard way or the easy way. Buy apple or pear marmalade or jam — or make your own. If using this receipt, you essentially boil your apples or pears tender, strain them, then clarify sugar to the ninth degrees and mix the liquid and apple or pear pieces into it. Let it cool and then put them in jars and refrigerate.

A Tart with a Marmalade of Apples

PARE some apples, cut them in four, take out the cores, cut them in small bits, put them in a stew-pan over the fire with a little water, some sugar, and a stick of cinnamon. When turned to a marmalade, rasp or grate into it some green lemon peel, let it be of a fine flavour and cold. Roll out some puff paste, and put it into a baking-pan, as large as the tart you design to make then put in your marmalade which you cover with paste, either cut into several forms, or in thin slips... Pippins are the best apples to make this sort of marmalade. (Borella)

Observations On Ices, Made With Ripe Fruits

The ices which we have just given you directions for, viz. Strawberry, Apricots, Raspberry, Currants, Peach, Anina, Cherry-Cream-Ices, must be first be made as it were for making them with the fruit alone; when they are so far prepared, you join your cream cold to them such as you buy it, for should you put it warm, as generally most of these fruits are acid, you would run the risk of making your cream turn directly into curds and whey; therefore you are to put your cream cold to your fruit; and if you want to have your ices very mellow, you must make use of the double cream which is thicker. — You may also make all those sorts of ices with the preserved fruit of each kind as we said in the directions, for the ices made with preserved fruits, by "putting your preserves in a bason, and mashing them well with a spoon, and the juice of four lemons and then the cream instead of water; for it is usual always to add some water to your fruit besides the lemon juice, in order to render them more fluid; now in the stead of that little water you put your cream to any quantity you please without bounds. (Borella)

NOTE: See Ice cream receipt. Anina is Pineapple

Royal Cream Ices

TAKE any quantity of cream, join to it yolks of eggs in proper proportion as we said in the pistachio nuts put a little half pounded coriander, cinnamon, orange, or lemon peel; add some pounded loaf sugar, and set it on the fire as we said before, till the moment you see it is going to boil; then pass it through the sieve and set it to ice as usual. (Borella)

NOTE: Essentially this is described as a certain type of ice cream flavored with pistachios, coriander, cinnamon, orange or lemon peel.

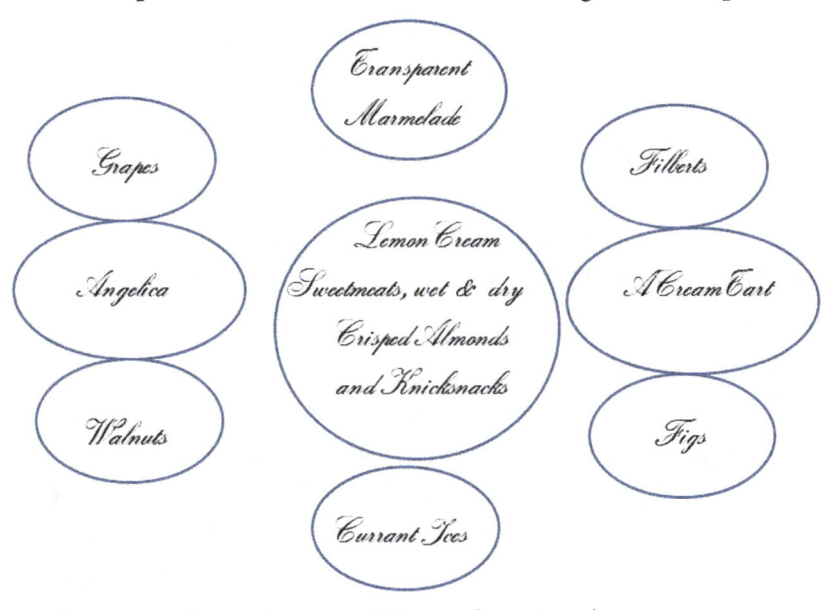

- Transparent Marmelade
- Grapes
- Filberts
- Angelica
- Lemon Cream Sweetmeats, wet & dry Crisped Almonds and Knicksnacks
- A Cream Tart
- Walnuts
- Figs
- Currant Ices

NOTE: I see figs, walnuts and filberts (hazelnuts) in season starting August/September timeframe.

Transparent Marmalade

TAKE very pale Seville oranges, cut them in quarters, take out the pulp, and put it into a bason, pick the skins and seeds out, put the peels into a little salt and water, let them stand all night, then boil them in a good quantity of spring water till they are tender, then cut them in very thin slices, and put them to the pulp, to every pound of marmalade put a pound and half of double refined sugar, beat fine, boil them together for twenty minutes; if it is not clear, and transparent, boil it five or six minutes longer, keep stirring it gently all the time, and take care you do not break the slices; when it is cold, put it in jelly or sweet-meat glasses: they are pretty for a desert of any kind. (Borella)

Sugared Grapes

TAKE any quantity of bunches of grapes which should not be quite ripe; make in every grape a small incision with a pen-knife to take the stones out, put them in a pan of water covered with cabbage leaves, and set them upon the fire, and proceed for the rest just as directed for the gooseberries, taking great care to keep the fire down and slow. (Borella)

NOTE: Many grapes today do not have "stones" and are seedless. It says to cover in cabbage leaves and simmer them on a low fire.

Moist Angelica

TAKE any quantity of angelica, it must be neither too green nor too ripe; to get it in its right point of maturity, as it is often later or sooner, sooner, agreeably to the difference of the season in which you cut it; the gardeners are the proper people to apply to; they can tell you in what season it must be gathered. There are generally two different times of gathering it, the second is always the best, which are commonly about the month of August, because it has then lost its greatest strength. You cut it in small pipes and boil it in water as much as you please, after which, you put it in fresh water in order to take with a knife the skin, which comes off very easily, and leave but the flesh which is under the skin you put it afterwards in the second degree of sugar, and proceed as for the other things as above mentioned. You may if you please squeeze six lemons in your sugar at the moment you put your angelica in; as it is a fruit naturally dry, it will better connect: the parts of the sugar together and prevent it from candying. (Borella)

NOTE: Angelica is a type of parsley that has celery type stalks. When reading about Angelica, I would recommend using celery versus an actual angelica plant.

Lemon Cream

TO a pint of water, add a pound of double refined sugar, and a piece of lemon-peel, set it on the fire to boil, and then let it stand till cold; beat up the whites of six eggs, and one yolk, with a tea-spoonful of orange-flower water, squeeze the juice of four lemons, stir all together, and strain it through a fine sieve into the syrup, take out the lemon peel, and set it over a gentle fire, stirring it one way till it is ready to boil, and taking off the scum as it rises, till it is as thick as cream; zest in a good deal of the peel, and put it into glasses. You may put in the glasses lemon-peel cut long and very thin. (Borella)

A Cream Tart

PUT in a Stew-pan two spoonfuls of fine flour, with the yolks of six eggs reserving the white of them. Mix your flower in a quart of milk, and season it with sugar and a stick of cinnamon, keep it stirring with a ladle, and put in a good lump of butter. Your cream being half done, put in some green lemon grated, some preserved lemon peel shred small with some bitter almond-biscuits, let the whole be thoroughly done. When ready, let it be cold, then put an abbess of puff paste in a baking pan with a border of paste, and put your cream over it, mix it with some orange flower-water and the white of eggs beaten up to snow; take care not to over-fill your custard, and let it be done either in the oven or under the cover of a baking pan, with fire under and over. When ready and glazed with sugar, by means of a red-hot fire-shovel, serve it up hot Cream tarts are made after the same manner. (Borella)

NOTE: Under cover of a baking pan is a bake kettle (dutch oven) with woods coals underneath and on top of the lid in which to bake.

To Pickle Walnuts Black

GATHER them when the sun is hot upon them, but try them with a pin to find if the shell is hard as they must be soft to run the pin through; put them in cold vinegar with a good deal of salt, let them stand three months, then boil up the vinegar with a little more salt, pour it on the pot; when cold boil them again till they are black, they then make a pickle for them thus; to two quarts of vinegar, half an ounce of mace, halt an ounce of cloves, an ounce of black pepper, the same of Jamaica ginger and long pepper, a table spoonful of flower of mustard put into a rag, two Ounces of common salt, boil it ten minutes, and pour it hot upon your walnuts: tie them down with a bladder they will be fit for use in six weeks. (Borella)

Currant Ices

TAKE currants picked from their stalks and squeeze them through a sieve, then take clarified sugar, boil it to the ninth degree, add your currant's juice, squeeze four lemons besides in it if you chuse, it will render them but the more mellow, strain them through a sieve a second time, and put them in the sabotieres to make them congeal, as we said for the lemons, to which I refer for the rest of the proceedings. (Borella)

Sugared Figs

TAKE some figs which should not be too ripe, prick them with a needle, put them in cold water, and set them on the fire till they become tender; then take them off and throw them into cold water; take the first degree of clarified sugar, put your figs in, and proceed as directed for the other preserves. (Borella)

Dessert Bills Of Fare

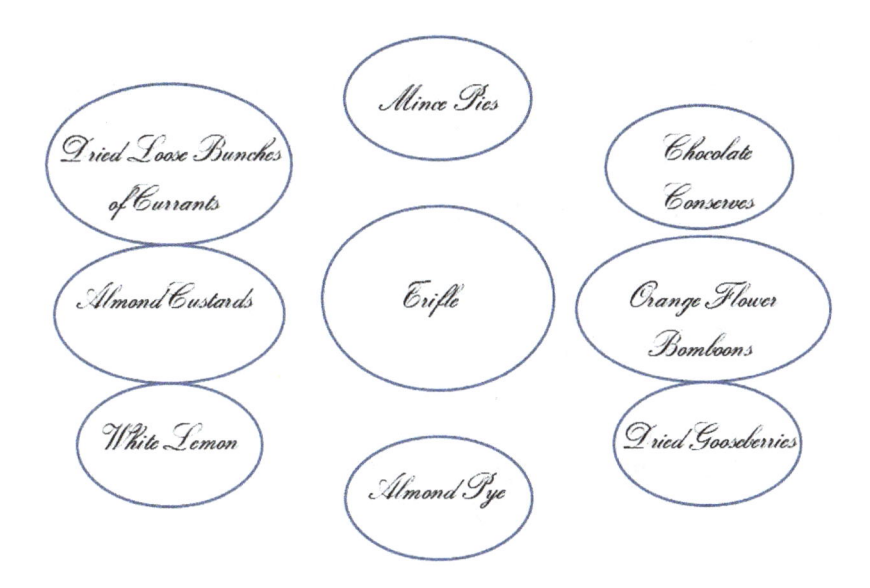

- Dried Loose Bunches of Currants
- Mince Pies
- Chocolate Conserves
- Almond Custards
- Trifle
- Orange Flower Bomboons
- White Lemon
- Almond Pye
- Dried Gooseberries

To Make Minced Meat

PARE and core pippins, till you have got pound; add of beef suet a pound, and raisins stoned half a pound; chop these very fine; take candied orange, lemon, and citron, one ounce of each, a pound of currants washed clean, and rubbed in a cloth till dry; half a pound of sugar, and a little salt; cinnamon and mace a quarter of an ounce of each, finely beaten, and a quarter of a pint of red wine; shred the sweetmeats, but not very small; then mix all very well together, and put it close down into a pot for use. When you make your pies, squeeze a little orange into them. (Borella)

NOTE: You can purchase a fruit based or meat based mince meat in the grocery store if you so desire.

To Make Mince Pies Another Way

PARE and core two pounds of golden pippens; two pounds of suet clean picked, and two pounds of raisins of the sun stoned; chop these separately very fine add two pounds of currants washed, dried, and rubbed very clean in a cloth, put these ingredients together, into a large pan, strew in half an ounce of cinnamon beaten fine, a pound of lump sugar pounded, the peel of a lemon cut fine, the juice of a Seville orange, a gill of sack and a gill of brandy: Mix all these very well together; then put it down close in a pot; and lay over it writing paper dipped in brandy. When you make your pies, add sweetmeats to them, if you please; but you will find them exceedingly good without. (Borella)

NOTE: Suet is the raw fat of beef or mutton. It is still used in cooking and best purchased from the meat department of your grocery store or butcher. If you are a vegetarian, you can use lard (fat) or butter. Do not use margarine.

To Make Minced Pies For Lent

BOIL six eggs hard, a dozen of golden pippens pared and cored, a pound of raisins of the sun stoned; chop these separately very fine & pound of currants washed, cleaned, and rubbed in a cloth, two ounces of sugar pounded, an ounce of citron, and an ounce of candied orange, both cut small, a quarter of an ounce of beaten cinnamon, two cloves beat fine, and half a nutmeg grated, a gill of canary, and half a gill of brandy; squeeze in the juice of Seville orange; mix these all well together, and press them close down into a pot for use. (Borella)

NOTE: Pippens are apples. Most raisins purchased in the store today do not have "stones" or seeds. Citron is described as a kind of lemon and can be purchased candied. Canary is a sweet wine from the Canary Islands.

Whole Currants

TAKE any quantity of currants, strip them of their stalks, pick off very carefully all those which happen to be squeezed, because these sticking themselves to those which are whole, that spoils them; then proceed as directed for the strawberries, except, you must not let them boil quite so long on the fire, being apt to burst; and, in order to give them greater consistence, instead of leaving them only twenty four hours, as you do, the strawberries in the sugar, you may leave the currants thus three days, because it is their nature to harden sugar. (Borella)

NOTE: Buy boxed dried currants usually sold near raisins, and hydrate them in water overnight and drain. Then proceed as directed

Coffee Conserves (Chocolate)
TAKE a little coffee ground; have a pan with a little clarified sugar in; boil it to the tenth degree, take it off from the fire, and proceed just the same way as we directed for the other conserves. The Chocolate Conserves, done in the same manner, with this difference only that you must dissolve your chocolate in a small pan over the fire before you add the sugar to it; or if you do, do not chuse to dissolve it, grate it with a grater very fine it will answer the same purpose. (Borella)

NOTE: A conserve is usually fruit cooked in sugar only long enough that the fruit is soft.

Almond Custards
TAKE a pint of cream, beat a quarter of a pound of blanched almonds fine, with two spoonfuls of orange flower water, sweeten it to your taste, beat up the yolks of two eggs, and stir all together one way; boil it over a gentle clear fire till it is thick, then pour it into a cup and bake it. (Borella)

NOTE: Orange flower water can usually be found in specialty grocery stores. Pour the mixture into ramekins or ceramic cups for baking.

To Make a Trifle
COVER the bottom of your dish with Naples biscuits broke in pieces, mackaroons and raatafla cakes, just wet them all with sack, pour on a good boiled custard when cold, then whipt syllabub over that. (Borella)

NOTE: Sack is usually a sweet Sherry. You can use a cold vanilla pudding versus a custard, and add whipt syllabub. If you do not have naples biscuit, you can use stale bread, make or purchase lady fingers. There are two receipts for Naples Biscuit in this book.

Lemon or Orange Bomboons

TAKE a piece of loaf sugar, rasp the oranges or lemons with it, what of them sticks to the sugar you brush off upon a paper; then you pound in a mortar that same piece of sugar, and put it in a pan with that which is upon the paper, and which tastes of the lemon or orange; you set it upon a gentle fire, in melting it slowly; after which you pour it upon a tin plate, which you must before have rubbed with a little buttery or it will stick to the plate; then you spread it with the rolling-pin as you did for the nuts; (observe the rolling-pin must likewise be rubbed with butter, for fear it should stick) when all that is done, and it is perfectly cold, then you cut it in what shape you please and send it up. (Borella)

NOTE: These are a lemon or orange flavored sugar candy. It tells you to use an orange or lemon and rub it on a sugar loaf and allow the sugar to fall off into a pan. You are supposed to do this for a pound of sugar, then melt it. Once it is melted, you put it on a plate that has been rubbed with butter and spread it out and let it cool. You can also do this with nuts to candy them.

White Lemon Conserves

This is made differently as follows; boil a pound of the finest sugar to the eight degree; take it off the fire, and squeeze the juice of a lemon in it, at different times, stirring continually; it will whiten the sugar as white as milk, if properly done, take care not to drop any of the seeds in it; work it well together, and pour it in the moulds, when it is mixed of an equal substance, which you will prove by pouring some with a spoon, as any other jelly. (Borella)

NOTE: These are lemon sugar candies poured into molds and allowed to cool. Make sure you "grease" the mold with butter to make sure they do not stick.

Dessert Bills Of Fare

Almond Pye

GET a pound of sweet almonds skinned, pound them well, moisten them now and then with the white of egg. Beat up the white of eight eggs to snow, mix four of their yolks with Savoy biscuits, rasped green lemon-peel, preserved lemon peel cut small, and some crisped orange flower, or orange flower-water. This done, take your almonds out of the mortar, mix them with the aforesaid ingredients, sugar it and sweeten it moderately, add the beaten white of eggs, put it over your abbess with a border round ready done with puff-paste in a baking pan, and let it be baked. The rest being done, as said about those before, serve it up hot. (Borella)

NOTE: This receipt should be read through as it tells you to have a puff-paste in a baking pan. It does not tell you the size or shape of the pan, but you can experiment with it. It does tell you to use a pound of sweet almonds and moisten them with one egg white. Then to take eight egg whites whipped to a froth (or snow), taking four yolks, some Savoy biscuits, green lemon-peel, preserved lemon-peel, and some orange flowers or orange flower water for more flavor. Besides the almonds and eggs, you should season to taste with the rest. A Savoy biscuit is a small finger shaped sponge cake. See receipt below.

To make Savoy Biscuits

Take eight eggs, separate the whites from the yolks, and beat the whites till they are very high; then put your yolks in with a pound of sugar, beat this for a quarter of an hour, and when the oven is ready, put in one pound of fine flour, and stir it till it is well mixed; lay the biscuits upon the paper and ice them, only taking care the oven is hot enough to bake them speedily. (Glasse)

Another Way...

Take twelve eggs, leave out half the whites, beat them up with a small whisk, put in two or three spoonfuls of rose or orange flower water, and, as you beat it up, strew in a pound of double refined sugar well beat and finely sifted; when the eggs and sugar are as thick and white as cream, take a pound and two ounces of the finest flour that is dried, and mix with it; then lay it in long cakes, and bake them in a cool oven. (Glasse)

To make Naples Biscuits

Put three quarters of a pound of very fine flour to a pound of fine sugar sifted; sift it three times, then add six eggs well beat, and a spoonful of rose water; when the oven is almost hot, make them, but take care that they are not made up too wet. (Glasse)

To make Sponge Biscuits

Beat the yolks of twelve eggs for half an hour, then put in a pound and an a half of fine sugar, beat and sifted, whisk it well till you see it rise in bubbles, then beat the whites to a strong froth, and whisk them well with the sugar and yolks; beat in a pound of flour, with the rind of two lemons grated, butter your tin moulds, put them in, and sift fine powder sugar over them; put them in a hot oven, but do not stop the mouth of it at first; they will take half an hour baking. (Glasse)

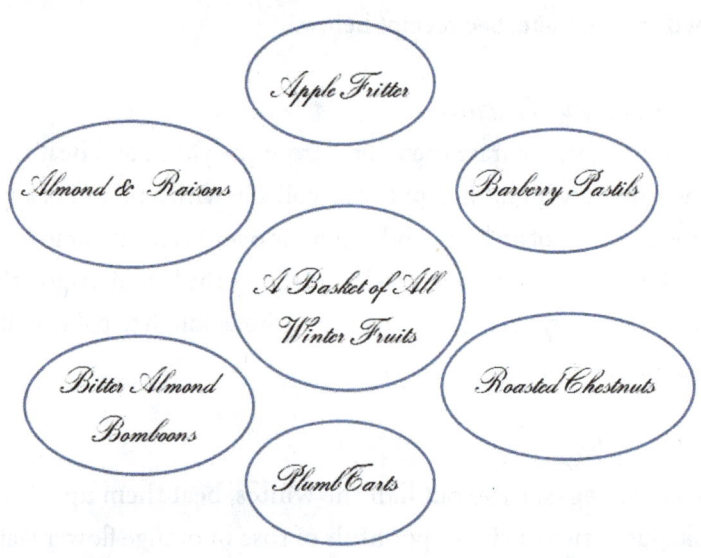

- Apple Fritter
- Almond & Raisons
- Barberry Pastils
- A Basket of All Winter Fruits
- Bitter Almond Bomboons
- Roasted Chestnuts
- Plumb Tarts

Apple Fritters

PARE the largest baking apples you can get, take out the core with an apple scraper, cut them in round slices, and dip them in batter, made as for common fritters, fry them crisp, serve them up with sugar grated over them, and wine sauce in a boat. They are proper for a side dish for supper. (Borella)

NOTE: Fry these in butter or lard. Depending on the time of year, you can also try Strawberry Fritters.

Strawberry Fritters

Make a paste with some flour, a spoonfull of brandy, half a glass of white wine, the whites of two eggs beat and green lemon shred fine. Mix it well, neither too thick nor too thin. It should rope in falling from a spoon. Dip some large strawberrys in to it, fry them and glaze them with a salamander. (Menon, French Family Cook)

NOTE: Fry these in butter or lard.

Barberry Pastils

TAKE a good quantity of barberries, strip them off the stalks; put to them a little watery to keep them from burning; boil them, and mash them as they boil, till they are very dry; then rub them through an hair sieve, and afterwards strain them through a strainer, that there may be none of the black noses in it; make it scalding hot, and to half a pint of the pulp put a pound of the sifted sugar; let it scald, and drop it on boards or glasses; then put it in a stove, and turn it when it is candied. (Borella)

NOTE: Dried barberries are available and edible and were used for a sour taste if lemons were not available. You can hydrate them in order to boil them as the receipt mentions.

Bitter Almond Bomboons

TAKE bitter almonds, boil them in water; take off their skin; after which you place them in the stove to dry them well, when they are well dryed, take a grater and do as we directed for the nuts; you must put the same weight of sugar as almonds. (Borella)

NOTE: These are a candied almond.

Plumb Tart

THE same management, with regard to boiling, must be observed with green or hard plumbs, and if large, must be split also; put a good quantity of sugar, both under and over: use the same paste as the last, with the top crust the same, and glaze it to give it a better look on the table; in regard to glazing any sorts of tarts, it is no farther necessary than agreeable, as many people like the crust, without its being glazed.

N. B. The kernels are seldom made use of. (Borella)

CHAPTER 8

The Tea Act, 1773, British Parliment

I felt it important to include a chapter totally dedicated to this act. Many know about it, but haven't actually read the act itself. It is provided here for you to read just as those in the time period did.

"An act to allow a drawback of the duties of customs on the exportation of tea to any of his Majesty's colonies or plantations in America; to increase the deposit on bohea tea to be sold at the India Company's sales; and to impower the commissioners of the treasury to grant licences to the East India Company to export tea duty-free.

WHEREAS by an act, made in the twelfth year of his present Majesty's reign, (intituled, An act for granting a drawback of part of the customs upon the exportation of tea to Ireland, and the British dominions in America; for altering the drawback upon foreign sugars exported from Great Britain to Ireland; for continuing the bounty on the exportation of British-made cordage; for allowing the importation of rice from the British plantations into the ports of Bristol, Liverpoole, Lancaster, and Whitehaven, for immediate exportation to foreign parts; and to impower the chief magistrate of any corporation to administer the oath, and grant the certificate required by law, upon the removal of certain goods to London, which have been sent into the country for sale;) it is amongst other things, enacted, That for and during the space of five years, to be computed from and after the fifth day of July, one thousand seven hundred and seventy-two, there shall be drawn back and allowed for all teas which shall be sold after the said fifth day of July, one thousand seven hundred and seventy-two, at the publick sale of the united company of merchants of England trading to the East Indies, or which after that time shall be imported, by licence, in pursuance of the said therein and hereinafter mentioned act, made in the eighteenth year of the reign of his late majesty King George the Second, and which shall be exported from this kingdom, as merchandise, to Ireland, or any of the British colonies or plantations in America, three-fifth parts of the several duties of customs which were paid upon the importation of such teas; which drawback or allowance, with respect to such teas as shall be exported to Ireland, shall be made to the exporter, in such manner, and under such rules, regulations, securities, penalties, and forfeitures, as any drawback or allowance was then payable, out of the duty of customs upon the exportation of foreign goods to Ireland; and with respect to such teas as shall be exported to the British colonies and plantations in America, the said dreawback or allowance shall be made in such manner, and under such rules, regulations, penalties, and forfeitures, as any drawback or allowance payable out of the duty of customs upon foreign goods exported to foreign parts, was could, or might be made, before the passing of the said act of the twelfth year of his present Majesty's reign, (except in such cases as are otherwise therein provided for:) and whereas it may tend to the benefit and advantage of the trade of the said united company of merchants of England trading to the East Indies, if the allowance of the drawback of the duties of customs upon all teas sold at the publick sales of the said united company, after the tenth day of May, one thousand seven hundred and seventy-three, and which shall be exported from this kingdom, as merchandise, to any of the British colonies or plantations in America, were to extend to the whole of the said duties of customs payable upon the importation of such teas; may it therefore please your Majesty that it may be enacted; and be it enacted by the King's most excellent majesty, by and with the advice and consent of the lords spiritual and temporal, and commons, in this present parliament assembled, and by the authority of the same, That there shall be drawn back and allowed for all teas, which, from and after the tenth day of May, one thousand seven hundred and seventy-three, shall be sold at the publick sales of the said united company, or which shall be imported by licence, in pursuance of the said act made in the eighteenth year of the reign of his late majesty King George the Second, and which shall, at any time hereafter, be exported from this kingdom, as merchandise, to any of the British colonies or plantations in America, the whole of the duties of customs payable upon the importation of such teas; which drawback or allowance shall be made to the exporter in such manner, and under such rules, regulations, and securities, and subject to the like penalties and forfeitures, as the former drawback or allowance granted by the said recited act of the twelfth year of his present Majesty's reign, upon tea exported to the said British colonies and plantations in America was, might, or could be made, and was subject to by the said recited act, or any other act of parliament now in force, in as full and ample manner, to all intents and purposes, as if the several clauses relative thereto were again repeated and re-enacted in this present act.

And whereas by one other act made in the eighteenth year of the reign of his late majesty King George the Second, (intituled, An act for repealing the present inland duty of four shillings per pound weight upon all tea sold in Great Britain; and for granting to his Majesty certain other inland duties in lieu thereof; and for better securing the duty upon tea, and other duties of excise; and for pursuing offenders out of one county into another,) it is, amongst other things, enacted, That every person who shall, at any publick sale of tea made by the united company of merchants of England trading to the East Indies, be declared to be the best bidder for any lot or lots of tea, shall, within three days after being so declared the best bidder or bidders for the same, deposit with the said united company, or such clerk or officer as the said company shall appoint to receive the same, forty shillings for every tub and for every chest of tea; and in case any such person or persons shall refuse or neglect to make such deposit within the time before limited, he, she, or they, shall forfeit and lose six times the value of such deposit directed to be made as aforesaid, to be recovered by action of debt, bill, plaint, or information, in any of his Majesty's courts of record at Westminster, in which no essoin, protection, or wager of law, or more than one imparlance, shall be allowed; one moiety of which forfeiture shall go to his Majesty, his heirs and successors, and the other moiety to such person as shall sue or prosecute for the same; and the sale of all teas, for which such deposit shall be neglected to be made as aforesaid, is thereby declared to be null and void, and such teas shall be again put up by the said united company to publick sale, within fourteen days after the end of the sale of teas at which such teas were sold; and all and every buyer or buyers, who shall have neglected to make such deposit as aforesaid, shall be, and is and are thereby rendered incapable of bidding for or buying any teas at any future publick sale of the said united company: and whereas it is found to be expedient and necessary to increase the deposit to be made by any bidder or bidders for any lot or lots of bohea teas, at the publick sales of teas to be made by the said united company; be it enacted by the authority aforesaid, That every person who shall, after the tenth day of May, one thousand seven hundred and seventy-three, at any publick sale of tea to be made by the said united company of merchants of England trading to the East Indies, be declared to be the best bidder or bidders for any lot or lots of bohea tea, shall, within three days after being so declared the best bidder or bidders for the same, deposit with the said united company, or such clerk or officer as the said united company shall appoint to receive the same, four pounds of lawful money of Great Britain for every tub and for every chest of bohea tea, under the same terms and conditions, and subject to the same forfeitures, penalties, and regulations, as are mentioned and contained in the said recited act of the eighteenth year of the reign of his said late Majesty.

And be it further enacted by the authority aforesaid, That it shall and may be lawful for the commissioners of his Majesty's treasury, or any three or more of them, or for the high treasurer for the time being, upon application made to them by the said united company of merchants of England trading to the East Indies for that purpose, to grant a licence or licences to the said united company, to take out of their warehouses, without the same having been put up to sale, and to export to any of the British plantations in America, or to any parts beyond the seas, such quantity or quantities of tea as the said commissioners of his Majesty's treasury, or any three or more of them, or the high treasurer for the time being, shall think proper and expedient, without incurring any penalty or forfeiture for so doing; any thing in the said in part recited act, or any other law, to the contrary notwithstanding.

And whereas by an act made in the ninth and tenth years of the reign of King William the Third, (intituled, An act for raising a sum not exceeding two millions, upon a fund, for payment of annuities, after the rate of eight pounds per centum per annum; and for settling the trade to the East Indies,) and by several other acts of parliament which are now in force, the said united company of merchants of England trading to the East Indies are obliged to give security, under their common seal, for payment of the duties of customs upon all unrated goods imported by them, so soon as the same shall be sold; and for exposing such goods to sale, openly and fairly, by way of auction, or by inch of candle, within the space of three years from the importation thereof: and whereas it is expedient that some provision should be made to permit the said company, in certain cases, to export tea, on their own account, to the British plantations in America, or to foreign parts, without exposing such tea, to sale here, or being charged with the payment of any duty for the same; be it therefore enacted by the authority aforesaid, That from and after the passing of this act, it shall and may be lawful for the commissioners of his Majesty's treasury, or any three or more of them, or the high treasurer for the time being, to grant a licence or quantity of licences to the said united company, to take out of their warehouses such quantity or quantities of tea as the said commissioners of the treasury, or any three or more of them, or the high treasurer for the time being, shall think proper, without the same having been exposed to sale in this kingdom; and to export such tea to any of the British colonies or plantations in America, or to foreign parts, discharged from the payment of any customs or duties whatsoever; any thing in the said recited act, or any other act to the contrary notwithstanding.

Provided always, and it is hereby further enacted by the authority aforesaid, That a due entry shall be made at the custom-house, of all such tea so exported by licence, as aforesaid, expressing the quantities thereof, at what time imported, and by what ship; and such tea shall be shipped for exportation by the proper officer for that purpose, and shall, in all other respects, not altered by this act, be liable to the same rules, regulations, restrictions, securities, penalties, and forfeitures, as tea penalties, &c. exported to the like places was liable to before the passing this act: and upon the proper officer's duty, certifying the shipping of such tea to the collector and comptroller of his Majesty's customs for the port of London, upon the back of the licence, and the exportation thereof, verified by the oath of the husband or agent for the said united company, to be wrote at the bottom of such certificate, and sworn before the said collector and comptroller of the customs, (which oath they are hereby impowered to administer,) it shall and may be lawful for such collector and comptroller to write off and discharge the quantity of tea so exported from the warrant of the respective ship in which such tea was imported.

Provided nevertheless, That no such licence shall be granted, unless it shall first be made to appear to the satisfaction of the commissioners of his Majesty's treasury, or any three or more of them, or the high treasurer for the time being, that at the time of taking out such teas, for the exportation of which licence or licences shall be granted, there will be left remaining in the warehouses of the said united company, a quantity of tea not less than ten millions of pounds weight; any thing herein, or in any other act of parliament, contained to the contrary thereof notwithstanding."

CHAPTER 9

Measures

A fourth part of the Weight of Marrow	½ cup or 4 ounces
As Thin as a Shilling	About 1/8 inch
As will lay on half a Crown	About one tablespoon
As will lay on a Six-Pence	About 1/4 teaspoon (what will fit on a dime)
Basin (of milk)	Depends on the size of thebasin (or bowl), generally 1 cup or 8 ounces
Butter the size of an egg	¼ cup
Butter the size of a Walnut	2 tablespoons
Coffee Cup	1 cup
Cut them cross-ways, as fine as a good big thread	About 1/8 inch
Dash	¼ teaspoon
Dash of Pepper	1/8 teaspoons
Dessert Spoon	2 teaspoon
Dish	1 pound (for butter)
Dozen	12
Dram	¾ cup or 1/8 fluid ounce
Drachm	½ tablespoon (liquid or dry)
Drops	60 equals ¾ teaspoon
Gallon	4 quarts, 8 pints
Gill	½ cup

155

¼ Gill	2 tablespoons
½ Gill	4 tablespoons or ¼ cup
Grated Lemon Rind	1 tablespoon
Grated Orange Rind	3 tablespoons
Faggot	A Bundle
Half Crown	2.29mm or .09 inch (thin)
Half Glass	Not a full glass
Handsome	Generous, thick, neatly trimmed
Jole	the head of a fish, the face, the cheek
Kitchen Cup	1 cup
Knob	A Lump (1 or 2 Tablespoons)
Large as a Walnut	See Size of a Walnut
Lump of Butter	2 tablespoons
Mutchkin	4 Gills
Ounce	2 tablespoons
Peck	8 quarts (4 cups in a quart or 32 cups, ½ peck is 16 cups, and ¼ peck is 8 cups)
Pinch	¼ teaspoon
Pinch of Salt	1/8 teaspoon
Pint	2 cups
Pint of Eggs	8 large, 10 medium, 12 small
Pound of Butter	2 cups (half a pound is 1 cup, ¼ pound is ½ cup)
" " Candied Fruit	1-1/2 cups
" " Corn Meal	3 cups (coarse), 4 cups (fine)
" " Dried Beans	2 cups
" " Eggs	8 to 9 large, 10 medium, 12 small
" " Flour	3 to 3-1/2 cups (white), 3-1/2 (whole wheat), 5 cups (rye)
" " Ground Suet	4 cups
" " Milk	2 cups
" " Oatmeal	4 cups
" " Powdered Sugar	2-1/2 cups
" " Sugar	2 to 2 ½ cups
Pugil	A little handful or big pinch
Quart	2 pints or 4 cups

Measures

Quart of Eggs	16 large, 20 medium, 24 small
Quartern	A gill, a quarter of a pint
Salt Spoon	¼ teaspoon
Scruple	¼ teaspoon
Size of a Fist	The size of the cook's fist
Size of a Goose Egg	9 inches or less
Size of a Walnut	Depends on the walnut, normally about 2 inches round
Spoonful	A teaspoon
Teaspoon	A common small spoon normally used in taking tea and equates to ½ teaspoon
Tablespoon	3 teaspoons
Teacup	¾ cup
Thick as a Crown (Big as a Crown Piece)	About 1-1/2 inch.
Thick as your Finger	Depends on the size of the cook's finger, normally ½ inch
Thickness of a French Roll	A French roll was normally ¼ to ½ inch thick
Thickness of Two Crown Pieces	About 6mm, one piece being 3mm or 3/32 inch which is just under ⅛ inch
Thimble Full	Depends on the size of the thimble, about 1 teaspoon
Two Quails	About 4-5 inches
Wine Glass	4 tablespoons, 1 gill, or ¼ cup

CHAPTER 10

Cooking Terms & Definitions

Apron — the fat skin covering the belly of a goose (or fowl).
Bake — to cook food in an oven or bake kettle, surrounding it with dry heat or hardening by means of heat.
Barbecue — to cook slowly near coals for several hours, turning it occasionally, and basting with liquid to season and keep it moist.
Baste — to drip, spoon, or brush meat or made dishes as it cooks with butter, a sauce, meat drippings, or fat to keep it moist.
Batter — a mixture of flour, eggs, &c., beaten together until it becomes a pap.
Beat (Beaten) — to stroke or hit in a particular manner (sometimes in a mortar)
Bedaub — to smear or cover with something, usually a sticky substance.
Bilge — to spring a leak by striking against something.
Bind — (it hard) to confine in bonds, to tie up.
Blacken — to make black or darken.
Blanched — made white and easier to peel by pouring boiling water over it and covering.
Bloat — to make something swell.
Blown — let the sugar boil longer than pearled, and if on blowing strongly through the holes of a skimmer after boiling little bladders appear, it is boiled to the degree called blown.

Boil — heating liquid until bubbles break on the surface. To "boiled to a marmalade" would be to boil until it became thick somewhere between a jelly and paste. To "boil high" would be to boil on a high heat for a number of minutes.

Bone — **(or Debone)** to take the bones out of anything.

Broth — liquid made by boiling bones to make a stock

Broyle — also to grill, to cook food directly under or above the heat source.

Brush — an instrument used to clean, sweep, or rub something (as in brushing a liquid on meat), to skim lightly.

Burn — to over cook food to where it is unpalatable and ruined.

Butter — to add butter, to boil butter until it turns brown, to rub butter on meat to prevent burning.

By Degrees — adding something gradually.

Calcined — to reduce to a substance easily powdered, normally burning to a calk (substance left when a metal or mineral combusts).

Candy — to cook, preserve, saturate, or coat with sugar or syrup.

Carmelized — having boiled sugar longer than crackled, dip a skewer into it and immediately after into cold water; it will snap the very instant it touches the cold water and must be taken off directly to prevent burning and discoloration, it is boiled to the degree called carmelized.

Caveack (Caveach) — pickling process for fish.

Chop — to cut with a quick blow, to cut into small pieces.

Clammy — glutinous or ropy, cold and moist.

Clear — bright, transparent, clear, serene (normally referred to broths or a clear fire (no smoke)).

Close — normally referred to tying a bag with string for a pudding very tightly so that it remains inside.

Codle (Coddle/Caudle) to boil gently, parboil, stew (fruit), thick (drink).

Collar — to roll meat (boned) up into itself after it is stuffed, larded, or seasoned.

Collops — a slice of meat fried or broiled, cooked quickly.

Conserve — sugar cooked together with fruit and nuts into a thick mixture.

Cover it Close — to lay one thing over another (normally to tighly cover a pot with a lid).

Clarify (Drawn) — for unsalted butter, melted where the water and milk solid separate and the golden liquid on the surface is used and foam is skimmed off. For sugar, to make clear, dissolved, and into a liquid. (See end of this section on how to clarify sugar and its degrees)

Coffin — moulds or cases of raised hot-water paste used as containers for dishes, pies, to cheesecakes. At times shaped like a box or coffin.

Compote — normally fruit that has been cooked slowly in sugar.

Congeal — fixed with cold, turned into ice.

Cordial — "A medicine to cheer the heart, a medicine that rallies the spirits, any thing that comforts." (Ash)

Core — the heart, the inside (as in to take out the inner part of the inside).

Corn — to cure (in salt or brine).

Crackled — the sugar having boiled longer than being feathered, dip a skewer into it, and immediately after into cold water; if on drawing the sugar from the skewer it snaps like glass, it is boiled to the degree called crackled.

Cream — to beat a mixture of ingredients until it is soft and smooth.

Crumble — broken into small pieces or reduced to bits.

Curdle (Curdling) — to coagulate or separate.

Cube (Cut Into Dice) — multiplied twice into itself, cut into small squares.

Cut (Half, Bits, Quarter, Cube) — to divide with or as with a sharp-edged instrument (i.e., cut in halves, cut into bits or small pieces as with butter, cut into dice).

Daub — to smear with some glutinous matter, to lay on with great abundance.

Display — spreading abroad.

Dobe (Daube) — from the French daubière or a covered casserole.

Dog Days of Summer — the hottest days of the summer, in Virginia that is early July into August.

Draw — to remove something, i.e., entrails from a bird or fish or to clarify butter (drawn).

Dredge — to lightly coat food to be fried, roasted, broiled, etc., also "to roll."

Dress — to prepare or make food for cooking.

Dry — to lay out until all moisture is taken from the object (i.e., meat, fruit, &c.)

Dust — to sprinkle (normally with flour, sugar, water, etc.).

Farce (Force) — to stuff or sometimes refers to forming meat into shapes or placed into patty-pans.

Feathered — when boiling sugar to a higher degree than blown, having dipped the skimmer in the sugar and shaken it over the pan, give it a sudden flirt behind you, when if it flies from the skimmer in particles resembling a feather, it is boiled to this degree.

Fillet – meat rolled and tied together.

Fine — to ornament, to decorate, to make clear, to make transparent, to purify.

Flat them Well — to level or depress (normally referred to tenderizing or beating meat.)

Flavored — to add something to a dish, thus changing or adding to the taste of that which you added.

Florendine (Florentine) — a covered pie or tart with puff paste, often with meat, with spinach, or custard.

Flour — to roll something, usually a piece of meat, in flour.

Fluff — soft and light.

Flummery — a creamy confection or pudding baked with or on oatmeal, barley, rice flour, or wheat bran.

Freeze — to be at a degree of temperature at which ice forms or liquids change to a solid state.

Freshen — to remove salt from preserved food by soaking it in several changes of water.

Fricando — a ragout, fricassee, or fancy dish of meat.

Fricassee — a dish composed of several ingredients in a broth.

Fritter — small cakes fried in lots of fat.

Frizzle — to cut meat very thin and then fry until it curls.
Froth — To baste meat (fowl) with fat or butter and dust it with flour before or as it is roasting so that the skin stays moist, to whip up into a foam.
Frowy — normally used in reference to butter gone musty or rancid.
Fry — to cook food in hot fat over moderate to high heat.
Gardenfluff — the produce of the garden especially those dressed and eaten with meat.
Garnish — to decorate, ornament, to set off a dish with something laid round it.
Gobbets — bite sized chunks or pieces
Grate — to rub to powder with a coarse kind of file or reduce something into small particles using a serrated surface called a rasp or grater.
Grillade — to broil.
Grilling — another term for broiling.
Ground — to crush into powder.
Harrico — highly flavored dish containing several ingredients.
Hard — firm or solid.
Hash — to cut food into small pieces.
High — tall, rising, elevated as in "done high."
Hull — to take off the husk (or clear away the outer covering).
Infuse — to pour in, to instill, to keep in any liquor with a gentle heat.
Jugged — to place in a "jug" or larger pan/jug of boiling water without the risk of the water getting into it.
Keep — to remain in a certain state (for a certain period of time).
Knead — To mix and work into a uniform mass, as by folding, pressing, and stretching with the hands.
Large Spoonful —
Lard — to thread strips of fat, bacon, onion, &c., into pieces of meat by using a type of needle or "larding pick."
Lid (Coffin Lid) — the paste to cover pies.
Lift — to raise.
Little — salt, butter, flour to taste or season.

Cooking Terms & Definitions

Loose — normally referred to tying a bag with string for a pudding or soup freely or not so tight.

Low — (oven) a fire or with little heat but enough to cook evenly.

Make (Made) — a term used for a dish of several ingredients, usually highly seasoned and garnished, or can be used when making drinks (cordials, syllabubs, and wines).

Marinade — a seasoned liquid in which foods such as meat, fish, and fruit are soaked in order to absorb the flavor or be tenderized.

Marmalade — The pulp of quinces boiled into a consistence with sugar (Ash, Vol I). This can be the pulp or any flesh of fruit boiled with sugar and thickened. Also known as Marmalet.

Mash — to depress, to flatten.

Merry-thought — the forked bone (wishbone) on a fowl.

Mince — to cut food into very small pieces.

Mix — to combined ingredients together.

Mock — to mimick, to imitate.

Moderate — (oven) 350-400 degrees Fahrenheit

Moisten — to wet in a small degree, to make damp.

Neat — elegant and clean, also known as a cow or ox.

Notch — to make an incision.

Pap — a thin kind of food for children made from bread and boiled in water or a fine pulp.

Parboil — to boil thoroughly.

Pare — cutting off from the surface.

Pearled — in boiling sugar, having dipped your finger into the sugar, then put your finger and thumb together and if on separation a string adheres to both, it is boiled to the degree called pearled.

Peel — to take off the rind or flay. A utensil used to take bread out of the oven.

Pelt — left in the fur

Pick — to take up, to gather, to separate, to clean.

Pickle — food that has been preserved in seasoned brine or vinegar and can be sour, sweet, hot, or flavored.

Pinch — a portion, normally herbs or spices, picked up between two to three fingers and added.

Plank — food, usually meat and fish, is cooked by baking or broyling on a wooden board.

Plain — with no decoration.

Plumped (soaked) — fattened or full of flesh as in rehydrating dried fruits and vegetables in water.

Poach — to boil slightly, to stab or pierce.

Porpetone (Porcupine) — a form in which meat was dressed, usually larded all over with small strips of red lean ham, white fat bacon, and green pickled cucumber and slowly stewed so that is appearance when it reached the table recalled that of the earlier "urchins."

Pott — to preserve salted or seasoned food in a pot or jar.

Prepare — to make, to get ready.

Preserve — to prepare foods so they can be kept longer without spoiling. This is done by salting, smoking, dehydrating, sugaring, putting into alcohol, or pickling.

Pretty Dish — neat, elegant.

Puff — fritter or small cake fried in fat

Pulp — any soft mass, the soft part of fruit or vegetables.

Pupton — a pate, ragout, or type of ground meat, fruit, or vegetables.

Quick — (oven, as possible) speedily or readily, fast. 425-450 degrees Fahrenheit

Quill — a feather where the shaft is sharpened at the end and used for writing with ink.

Ragoo (Ragout) — a sort of stew to which a highly flavored or seasoned sauce was added near the end of cooking time.

Raised — a pie with a very thick, heavy crust designed to contain a filling (not usually eaten).

Rancid — gone bad.

Rasher — A thin piece of meat (i.e., rasher of bacon).

Rasp — to grate (raspings are breadcrumbs).

Reduced by Half — boil the liquid until is if half of what was originally put in.

Render — term used to describe chopping, melting, and skimming suet or lard for use.

Rinsed — to wash or cleanse by washing.

Roast — to oven cook food in an uncovered pan so that the exterior is browned and interior tender and moist.

Roll — to move food around in a circle, to wrap, to form by rolling.

Rub — to touch over as to leave something behind, normally in reference to meat.

Salt — there was white, Yorkshire, Maldern, and bay salt all made from the evaporation of sea water. Food was salted by adding salt to it in order to preserve it.

Sauté — to brown vegetables or meat in butter or oil

Season (Season it High) — add extra spices and herbs.

Scald — to burn with hot liquor or liquids.

Scallop — to prepare food by layering it.

Scoop — to cut hollow, to empty by a ladle, to take out and make hollow.

Scorch — burn as to harden the surface, to become dry due to heat, to burn superficially.

Scotch — a slight surface cut, usually a notch or score of flesh or fish.

Scrape — to take off the surface by the light action of a sharp instrument (usually a knife), to clean off the surface.

Season — to flavor foods.

Sew it Up — to use a needle and thread to close something up.

Shred — to cut in small pieces or fragments.

Sift — to separate by a sieve, to part.

Skim (Skum) — take off the top.

Simmer — to consistently cook liquid just before boiling.

Skin — a hide, pelt, or body covering. To strip off.

Sippet — a small piece of toast or fried bread used for dipping, in gravy, or soups.

Sirkin — (butter)

Slack (Slow) Oven — a weak or slow oven. 300-325 degrees Fahrenheit

Slice — to cut a piece of food into something smaller, usually thin.

Smoke — to treat meat, cheese, or fish for preserving by using a low fire.

Smooth — in clarifying sugar, after clarifying, having dipped your finger into the sugar, then put your finger and thumb together, if in opening them you see a small thread drawn that when it breaks immediately it leaves a drop on your finger, you may conclude the sugar is boiled to the degree of smooth.

Soaked — to place food into liquid, to lie steeped in moisture, to moisten, to drench.

Soft — void of hardness, flexible. In reference to a fire, very slow.

Solid — compact, dense, strong, firm.

Spread — to extend or expand, to cover by expansion, to stretch, to cover over.

Sprinkle — in small quantities.

Stake — a slice of meat to boil or fry.

Stale — long kept or altered by time.

Stew — to cook food barely covered with liquid and simmered slowly for a long period of time with a tightly covered lid.

Stringy — small cords or slender rope normally in reference to meat.

Stone — to take out the pit of fruit.

Stove — to stew.

Strain (Sieve) — to pass through a strainer, a name for the "threads" in egg whites, pole to clean out the bake oven.

Strong Enough to Bear an Egg — water that is boiled with salt to a degree that eggs will float.

Stuff — to put a mixture into meat.

Swab — to clean the surface of the bake oven floor before the food goes in or a wet cloth wrapped around a long

Cooking Terms & Definitions

Syrup — to boil something until it becomes thick (usually liquid with other ingredients).

Tear — to pull into pieces.

Tender — soft, easily impressed.

Thicken — condensed, to make close, to concentrate.

Thick as Cream — normally a term used when boiling a liquid (milk) with flour or other thickening agent to make it more concentrated.

Thigh — to cut up or carve (from the thigh).

Thin — slice, spread, to a small degree.

Toast — to heat something (normally bread) until it is brown on the outside and hard.

Treadles — air pockets or lumps.

Trim — to remove or put in a neat or orderly condition, to cut down into a required size or shape.

Truss — to affix a piece of meat or fowl on a spit or tied up for roasting.

Unbrace — Loosened or relaxed.

Undressed — not prepared., not ornamented.

Unlace — Freed from its confinement (as in removing bones from a fur or fowl).

Viand — food neatly dressed.

Walm — a bubble in boiling, a boiling up; can be counted as a second when boiling starts.

Wash — to cleanse by liquid (normally water).

Whipped — to strike with anything flexible, to drive with lashes (as in whipping cream to a froth with a wisk).

Working — for ice creams, scraping down the pot, turning the pot, and scraping again as it freezes. For dough, the act or process of moulding something pliable.

To Clarify Sugar — In proportion to three pounds of fine, lump, or powder sugar, which you are to put in a skillet or boiler; break into an earthen pan the white of an egg with near a pint of fresh water, and beat them up all together with your hand to a white froth; then put the whole into the copper kettle, or pan, and set them on a clear and slow fire ; when it begins to boil, do not fail to put a little more water in, and begin to skim it, till you see the scum is very white, the sugar become pretty clear; that done, to clear it properly, sift it in a wet napkin or silk sieve, and pass it thus into what vessel you please, till you want to make use of it.

FIRST DEGREE OF REFINING SUGAR.

I'be practition may take notice, that one pound of sugar is sufficient to make a trial of all the different degrees.

PUT the clarified sugar on a moderate but clear fire, to boil; you will know when it is to this first degree, by dipping one finger in it, and join it to another; by opening, if it draws to a small thread, and in breaking, returns to each finger in the nature of a drop, it is done.

Second degree, It is boiled a little more, and the thread extends further before it breaks, and is proved as the first.

Third degree, It is still boiled a little more, until it does not break, by extending the fingers half as much as is possible to do.

Fourth degree, It is boiled a little longer than the third; and is known to be the degree wanted, by not breaking, by all the extension that can be made with the fingers; and also when it forms in small pearls in the boiling, round and raised.

Fifth degree, It is known, by taking up some of the sugar with a skimmer, and dropping it in the boiling sugar again; if it forms a slanting streak on the surface.

Sixth degree, By a little more boiling, and tried in the same manner as the last.

Seventh degree, Which is known by dipping a skimmer into it; give it a shake, and blow through it directly; if it blows to small sparks of sugar, or kinds of small bladders, it is to the proposed qualification.

Eighth degree comes with a little more boiling, which is known by the same trial; the difference only is, that the sparks or bladders are to be larger, and of a stronger substance.

Ninth degree, Is known by dipping a stummer into it, and give it a turn over the hand; if it turns to large sparks, which clog together in the rising, it is done to this degree.

NOTE: A strummer can be a stick of any shape.

Tenth degree, Is done by a little more boiling, and proved by dipping two fingers in cold water, and directly into the sugar, and into cold water again; what sticks to your fingers, ought to roll up like a bit of paste, and to remain pretty pliant when cold.

Eleventh degree, Is proved by the last method, which, by a little more boiling, makes it harder.

Twelfth degree, Is known by the same method, as in the two last; the only difference is, that it ought to crumble between the fingers, being first dipped in cold water. (Borella)

CHAPTER 11

Of Colours for Confectionery

The colors used in confectionery are generally harmless; for though no one thinks of eating an ornament or figure, yet such colors as vermillion, verdigris, yellow ochre, and many others which are poisonous, should be avoided, if possible. The following come from the cookery book by Jarrin, with notes on if it should be used or not. Most of these are included to show what they used to color desserts and table centerpieces.

Colours Good to Eat

The colours fit to eat are cochineal, carmine diluted, saffron, spinach green, Prussian blue, and colours made with chocolate and caramel; caramel should be diluted with a little water, as it goes farther than the dry powder, yet in some cases it must be used dry, as in the royal iceing, and in articles for the small oven: saffron must be infused in hot water, consequently you must put the necessary quantity to your sugar a moment before it is done; it will require a few minutes more boiling, as the saffron will lessen the degree of heat; spinach green is to be used to colour opaque bodies; such as are transparent must be coloured with a little Prussian blue, mixed with yellow; if blue alone be wanted, it must be ground with a little water, taking care to use but a small quantity of it; browns may be made of chocolate, a strong decoction of coffee, or caramel burnt and dissolved in water; the violet colour is made with red and blue; orange with saffron and red; and the green with yellow and blue. (Jarrin)

NOTE: Caution must be taken when using any of these coloring agents today, in most cases, it is best NOT to. If an experiment is to be done using them, they should NOT be eaten.

To Choose Cochineal

Cochineal should be large, clean, heavy, dry, of a silvery shining colour, and, when bruised, of a dark red. (Jarrin)

NOTE: Cochineal is a scale insect of which can be purchased whole or powdered. It is used now for dyeing fabrics as well as in cosmetics. A water-soluble form is used in combination with various forms of carmine to color various drinks and edible foods.

Of Preparing Cochineal

Take an ounce of cochineal, pound it well, and make a soft lye with wood-ashes boiled in water; clear it off through a flannel bag; take a pint of it, let it boil up, and put in your cochineal; pound a quarter of an ounce of alum and a quarter of an ounce of cream of tartar, and add them to the cochineal; and reduce it by boiling, till it becomes of a very dark fine red; if it is for keeping, add pulverized sugar. You may use this colour in every thing, particularly in gum paste, compotes, preserves, jellies, ices, &c. (Jarrin)

Carmine

Carmine, No. 1, is the best, though the dearest; as the inferior article is generally adulterated with cinnabar; but you may easily manufacture carmine as follows: Take a boiler sufficiently large to contain two pails and a half of river water, perfectly clear; put it on the fire, and when it boils, shake in gently a pound of cochineal, ground in a new coffee mill; stir it with a clean hair pencil, and if the heat be too great, lesson your fire, and throw in a glass of cold water, that the cochineal may not boil over; let it boil for half an hour, then add an alkaline lye, prepared as follows: Boil three-quarters of an ounce of pulverized soda in two quarts of water, for eight or ten minutes; take it off, filter it, put it into your cochineal; let it boil up five or six times; take off the boiler, place it in a slanting position, that the cochineal may deposit; add to it three-quarters of an ounce of powdered alum, stir it well to dissolve the alum, and let it stand for twenty-five minutes. See if it takes a fine scarlet colour; pour off the liquor very gently into another clean boiler, and do not stir it much, to avoid dividing the deposit; beat up the whites of two eggs in a pint of water, pour it into the colour; stir it well, put the boiler on the fire, till it nearly boils; the whites of the eggs will coagulate, and precipitate with the colouring particles which are to form the carmine. Take the boiler off, and let the carmine settle for twenty-five minutes; pour off the liquid till you see the carmine at the bottom, which will be like thick milk; pour it into an earthen pan or bowl, strain it through a fine cloth to let the moisture run from it, and drain the carmine. You must strain the liquid several times till it is quite clear; when the carmine is drained, and has a proper consistence, take it up with a silver spoon, lay it on plates to dry in the stove, and, when dry, grind it on the stone. (Jarrin)

NOTE: Caution must be taken when using any of these coloring agents today, in most cases, it is best NOT to. If an experiment is to be done using them, they should NOT be eaten.

Vegetable Carmine

2 lb. Brazil-Wood, 2 oz. pulverized Cochineal, oz. Rock Alum, 15 oz. Sal Ammoniac, 1 oz. Salt, 1 lb. 12 oz. Nitric Acid, and 8 oz. Pewter Filings. Divide the alum into four parts, and boil the Brazilwood in eight pints of water, with the pulverized cochineal tied in a piece of cloth; when reduced to half, take it from the fire, put into it one of your parcels of alum; strain the decoction through a cloth, into a pan ; put back the chips on the fire with the same quantity of water: reduce it as at first; strain it off, and repeat

Of Colours for Confectionery

the same four times, putting one part of the alum each time. At the last boiling, add one quarter of an ounce of sal ammoniac, and put the whole together into a pan, keeping it warm. Put your nitric acid into a long-necked bottle, in which, on the previous evening, should have been dissolved one ounce of salt, and ounce of sal ammoniac; place it in a pan full of water; fix it so as not to move; warm the water more than lukewarm, and put in your pewter filings by small quantities, and continue this gradually as you see it dissolve. When the whole is dissolved, pour it into the decoction, mix it well, strain it through a cloth, and let it stand for twenty-four hours; then pour off the yellow water till you come to the colour; fill up your pan with clean water, and repeat this morning and evening for eight days, when you will find the water quite clear, leaving no salt or acid in the colour. Keep it in a pot for use, always having some clean water on it to preserve it in a liquid state.

NOTE: Caution must be taken when using any of these coloring agents today, in most cases, it is best NOT to. If an experiment is to be done using them, they should NOT be eaten.

Gamboge

This is a gum, and must be dissolved in cold, or lukewarm water, to colour gum paste. In large quantities, it would act as an emetic and cathartic.

NOTE: This is a yellow pigment. It is currently used to dye fabric.

Saffron

Must be infused in warm water; it should be chosen very dry and soft, in long shreds of a fine red colour, and of a pleasant balsamic taste: it is a good stomachic. (Jarrin)

NOTE: Saffron can be purchased in the grocery store and used as a yellow dye that is food safe.

Sap Green

This is prepared from the fruit of the buckthorn; it is in a hard paste, and must be dissolved in water for use, to paint gum paste; it is not good to eat in large quantities.

NOTE: It is best not to eat this at all. Ripe berries produce a pink dye, unripe berries produce a yellow dye.

Spinach Green

Take the necessary quantity of spinach, pound it well, and squeeze the juice through a cloth; put it in a pan, on a strong fire, stir it with a spoon, and as soon as you see it look curdy take it off the fire, and drain the liquor through a silk sieve; what remains on the sieve will be the colour. (Jarrin)

NOTE: Spinach is safe to eat.

Ivory Black

Is made with ivory cut in small pieces, and calcined in the fire in a covered pot or crucible, till it ceases smoking: it is only used to paint gum paste. (Jarrin)

NOTE: Real ivory is banned from use today.

Prussian Blue

Prussian blue is to be preferred by the confectioner, though it must be used sparingly: the turnsole and indigo afford a bad colour. (Jarrin)

NOTE: Prussian Blue's original source was supposedly ground bones and blood. There are substitutes out there that are now used in ink among other things, and should not be mixed in anything edible.

Bol Ammoniac

Is of a reddish colour, something like cinnamon, and used for gilding, or to paint gum paste, as well as brown umber, and bistre. (Jarrin)

NOTE: Also known as Armenian Bole, is a soft bright red clay found in Armenia and Tuscany.

Of Using Colours

The colours just mentioned are those used to paint gum paste; they are ground on a marble slab, and are moistened with water, and a little gum arabic dissolved and strained through a cloth, with a pinch of fine powdered sugar, or sugar candy; the gum is to fix the colour, and the sugar to make it shine; if you have no gum you may use isinglass, but then the colour must be warm. (Jarrin)

NOTE: Isinglass is a "gelatin" taken from the swim bladders of fish, particularly sturgeon, and used to make jelly, glue, and clarifying ale.

Of Decoration

The decoration of the table regards chiefly the arrangement of the Dessert, which should consist of Assiettes Monties, baskets of fruit and flowers, a variety of bonbons, porcelain figures, glass, &c. which should all be arranged with taste and elegance. The art of decoration was formerly carried to a great extent in France, immense sums were expended upon it, and many of the first artists in the different departments were employed; the whole, when completed, had the appearance of enchantment. The author is proud to enumerate among his friends, Messrs. Monprive-, Leccelan, and Cocard, who have executed decorations and embellishments for the table, which will probably never be surpassed. But this ornamental style of arranging the dessert is not much used in England, a few Assiettes Monties only being employed to decorate the table. Farewell, then, fine groupes, allegorical subjects, trophies, country sports, landscapes, and mythological emblems! Till better times shall arrive, we must content ourselves with the simple Assiettes Montees... (Jarrin)

On the Construction of Assiettes and Pieces Monties

To be a proficient in this part requires a general knowledge of the fine arts, particularly the principles of architecture; for without this, however well your piece may be finished with regard to workmanship, it still remains a dull, heavy, unmeaning mass, having no proportion nor a particle of true design in it. I have seen many pieces, and some in the principal shops, with these defects, although otherwise well executed. My limits will not allow me to enter into the details necessary to illustrate this part, therefore the artist must refer to books on the subject; but in the absence of these it is best to work from some correct drawing, which, with the few notes I shall subjoin, may serve for general purposes.

There are many prevailing styles or orders of architecture, as the Egyptian, Grecian, Roman, Saxon, Norman, Gothic, &c. The Gothic is the most beautiful, being pointed, and is generally used for cathedrals and churches. The Norman is plain and simple, with semicircular arches. The Saxon is after the same style, into which are introduced some ornamental workings. The Egyptian is more flat and square, embellished with hieroglyphics. In the Grecian and Roman architecture there are five orders, viz., Tuscan, Doric, Ionic Corinthian, and Composite; and a building may be denominated Ionic, Corinthian, &c., merely from its ornaments. The number of columns, windows, &c., may be the same in either order, but varied in their proportions. The height of the columns in each is, — for the Tuscan, seven times its diameter; Doric, eight; Ionic, nine; Corinthian, ten; Composite, ten. The Tuscan is quite plain, without any ornament whatever; the Doric is distinguished by the channels and projecting intervals in the frieze, called tryglyphs; the Ionic by the ornaments of its capital, which are spiral, and called volutes; the Corinthian by the superior height of its capital, and its being ornamented with leaves, which support very small volutes; the Composite has also a tall capital, with leaves, but is distinguished from the Corinthian by having the large volutes of the Ionic capital. The Grecian and Roman orders differ in some respects as to the style of each, but for particulars refer to works on the subject. These orders are adopted for buildings, with various modifications, in most parts of the world.

The Chinese have a peculiar kind of style, which needs no description, as it is generally represented in this country on our delft ware, &c, The Swiss style, which is something of the Gothic, is very well adapted for

Of Colours for Confectionery

pieces montees, as well as the Doric, Ionic, and Corinthian orders, they being more light and elegant. (Parkinson)

NOTE: Assiettes Montes are mounted plates or stacked cake stands as we know them today.

Of Pieces Montees

These are in general made to represent buildings of all descriptions, fountains, trophies, vases, cups, helmets, the last being generally mounted on pedestals and filled with flowers, fruit, &c.; also rocks, bridges, fortifications, &c. &c., the building, &c., being generally made with gum-paste, confectioners' or almond pastes. The bodies of rocks may be formed with pieces of rock sugar, cakes, biscuits, &c., of all descriptions, being fixed together with caramel sugar; those not intended to be eaten may be made with papier machee and common gum-paste; the rocks or bottoms of these are often formed with pieces of cork, flocks, and paper, the surface being afterwards covered with a coating of very thin icing, which is applied with a brush.

To construct your pieces with accuracy, first cut out your intended design in stout paper, in suitable parts to be put together; then roll out the paste thin on a marble stone; lay your pattern on it, and cut your paste to it with a small sharp-pointed knife; let it dry, and fix it together with some dissolved gum, or a little gum-paste made rather thin with water. Cut your ornaments or decorations from pasteboards; let them dry a few minutes, and fix them in their proper places.

Water may be represented with a piece of looking-glass, and falling water with silver web or spun glass. (Parkinson)

Margaret Tilghman Carroll by Charles Wilson Peale, 1770-1771
Courtesy of the Mount Clare Museum House

CHAPTER 12

Margaret Tilghman Carroll

When I started to write this book, I had owned a pamphlet compiled by the Colonial Dames of America in the State of Maryland originally published in 1963 and titled, *Some of Mrs. Carroll's Favorite Receipts."* I was intrigued since it is a pleasure to tie a recipe to a specific person. In this case, Mrs. Carroll's "account book" resides in the Maryland Historical Society where I went to take a look at it. What I found within was wonderful, although many pages had been cut out from the book. There were two styles of handwriting, or so it seemed, and several recipes located within. When comparing the receipts written in the book with cookery books of the time, most of the ones found are verbatim, so they are not specifically created by Mrs. Carroll. However, they were important enough to her to be written in her book, and I wanted to include some of them in mine. The other amazing thing to note is that she personally knew Charles Wilson Peale, who painted her and her husband's portraits, as they supported him in his craft. I have also found in my research, that Peale had worked for a short time as a silver smith, watch and maker (per the Maryland Gazette, February 9, 1764).

As I did more research, I decided to also dedicate my book to her so her time on this earth is highlighted and recognized other than those at Mount Clare. I also find the political climate at the time that I write this book seems to disparage some of our ancestors, founding fathers, and others who may have owned slaves. From what I have read about Margaret, she and her husband would have taken care of those they were responsible for to the best of their abilities just as General George Washington did. The political climate, social norms, the laws that they lived under were not what we know today. They were governed by different standards. I do not claim to know how they lived, why they lived in the way they did, and I certainly do not put my own 21st century mindset on how they did things. Our society has evolved so much in so many ways. What I was brought up to know and how I live and think today cannot be translated to anything even remotely related to the 18th century, but I do try to understand that time.

This is by no means a complete account of Margaret, which has been written in two excellent books entitled *"Mount Clare, Being an Account of the Seat built by Charles Carroll, Barrister, upon his Lands at Patapsco,"* by Michael F. Trostel, and *"Mistress of Mount Clare: The Life of Margaret Tilghman Carroll 1742-1817,"* Masters Thesis, University of Maryland Baltimore County, 2004, by Kimberly Moreno. I was able to get a copy of the first book, but not the second thesis. I'm highlighting some of her life here from the first source as well as my own research.

Born in 1742 in Talbot County, Maryland, Margaret was the daughter of Matthew Tilghman and Anne Lloyd. Margaret's father was a prominent patriot during the American Revolution and is credited as the father of Maryland's first Constitution and Bill of Rights. The Tilghman's lived on a plantation called "Bay Side" which is now called "Rich Neck Manor." The Tilghman's were a wealthy family, and Margaret inherited £4,000 from her Great Aunt Margaret Bennett Ward when she was only four years old. Her family has ties to the British throne through her grandmother, Henrietta Maria Neale (who was a godchild of Queen Henrietta Maria), and Margaret inherited a ring containing a miniature of Charles I when her mother passed away.

Margaret Tilghman Carroll

Margaret was 21 in 1763 when she married her 40 year old cousin, Charles Carroll, Esq. (who asked in his writings to be identified as "Barrister" so as to differentiate himself from the other Charles Carroll in Maryland — including his father Dr. Charles Carroll). They were married in Talbot County on June 23, 1763. Charles also came from a wealthy family. Margaret was described in the June 30, 1763 edition of the Maryland Gazette as a "young Lady of great Merit, Beauty, and Fortune." They had a house in Annapolis that abutted the Ridout House above the Harbor on Duke of Gloucester and Green Street, as well as their country home called "Mount Clare." This was not their only properties, but two of which I will mention and where I believe they spent a majority of their time.

Just after they were married, Charles made an order to his London agents, William and James Anderson (who were also cousins), which included "The Best Book of Cooking Published." This, of course, piqued my interest! Were some of the receipts she wrote down in her account book from this one? One of which is "Muffin Bread" of which is transcribed below —

~~~~~~~~~~~~~~~~~~~~

181

Muffin Bread

Original Receipt — "1 pint of Flour, 3 small eggs or two large ones, 1 oz. of Butter, 1 Teacup of new Milk, & 3 spoonsful of yeast. Beat your eggs very light warm your milk & stir your butter in it, when that is entirely melted & your eggs light, add it to them then beat in the flour by degrees, your yeast last & let it to rise where you do your bread."

This one is very easy except it does not describe what type of pan you bake it in, nor how hot the oven needs to be. They could have used a variety of leavening agents that included barm, beaten egg whites, or pearl ash. We will use brewer's yeast which makes it easy to find today. This adaptation was done by Zachary Long in the Daniel Boone Homestead Hearth Kitchen.

2 Cups of Flour	¾ cup of Milk
2 Large Eggs	1 packet of Dry Active Yeast
2 Tablespoons Butter	Preheat oven to 350 degrees.

Mix your yeast, flour, and salt together in a small bowl. Beat two large eggs very well and set aside. Warm your milk and butter together. Once the milk has warmed, and the butter is melted, add in your beaten eggs. Add flour mixture to wet ingredients, mix just to combine, batter will be lumpy and be very wet, its fine.

Grease and flour a bread pan or baking dish. Pour bread into greased pan and let rise for about 1-1/2 hours. It will rise half of its starting volume.

Bake bread for about 30 mins, bread will be light brown in color. Serve while warm with a sweet jam or sweet butter. (The addition of ½ teaspoon of salt to the flour mixture will help the taste of the bread.)

Margaret was also very interested in gardening, and Mount Clare was a plantation that allowed her to practice what seemed to be her passion. Charles made several orders to the Andersons in London for various items to include seeds for broccoli, cabbage, celery, peas, sorrel, colly flowers, cantaloupe, and asparagus. They also requested on July 2, 1768 some plumb, apricot, nectarine, cherry, pear trees, and Peach stones. The order also included "1/4 Chest best Lisbon Lemons by your first Ship and ¼ Chest by your Last" among many other items…and specified that "I would have all the above trees 3 years old from Graft or Bud if Can be Safely moved or as old as they Can be moved." Charles also refers to Margaret in his letters for these requests as "Peggy."

With the request for peach stones, we can assume that peach trees were grown at Mount Clare. Within Mrs. Carroll's account book there is a receipt for "Peach Cordial." Cordial and "Waters" were sometimes used together or independently. I did a cursory glance at several cookery books and did not specifically find a receipt for this one. It may be that there is a similar receipt and peaches were substituted in it. In the 1775 dictionary by John Ash, a cordial is defined as "A medicine to cheer the heart, a medicine that rallies the spirits, any thing that comforts."

It is transcribed as follows —

Peach Cordial
"Take 3 doz ripe peaches, wipe them and peel them into a stone jar — add 3 lb of loaf sugar clarified with an egg, pour over them one gallon of boiling water, then add two gallons of old peach or apple Brandy — one handful of peach kernels, and a little all spice, shake them frequently. They will be fit to use on New Year's day."

NOTE: In order to make this exactly as written, a breakdown of the receipt must be done. It can also be cut in half if you do not want to make as much. The original recipe calls for 3 dozen ripe peaches, 3 pounds of clarified sugar, 2 gallons of peach or apple brandy, peach kernels, allspice. In this receipt, we will purchase the peach or apple brandy.

I decided to make a third of this receipt. I took 12 peaches (1 dozen), 1 pound of sugar, 1 tablespoon allspice (I used "kitchen pepper" of which the receipt is in A Book of Cookery by a Lady and below), and 8 cups of apple brandy. I left out the peach kernels.

Clean and peel 1 dozen ripe peaches. Add them to large enough containers to hold at least a gallon, be it stone containers or large glass mason jars. Then take 1 pound of clarified sugar (see below to make the sugar.) Then add 8 cups of peach or apple Brandy to it. Add some handful of peach kernels if you so desire (which is the inside of the peach stone or pit), and Allspice to taste. Then mix it together. Shake frequently over the course of 3 to 6 months. Since it mentions that it will be fit "for use" on New Year's day, this would have been made when peaches were generally in season from July through September.

To clarify the Sugar — The rule of thumb is to take ½ pint (2 cups) of water to each pound of sugar, and one egg white per 2 pounds of sugar. So, take the white of one egg, beat it smooth, and mix it into 1/2 pint of water. Then add your sugar and let it sit to soften a little before you set it on the fire (or stove); stirring until the sugar is dissolved. Bring it to a boil and there will be "scum" that is essentially the egg white that rises. Once you see the "scum," immediately put in some cold water and it will stop boiling. Bring it to a boil again, and take it off the fire and let it settle. Pour it into a hair sieve (or strain it) into another pan. Take the strained solution and put it in your jar(s).

~~~~~~~~~~~~~~~~~~~~

Kitchen Pepper (Another Way)

MIX together two ounces of the best white ginger, an ounce of black pepper, an ounce of white pepper, an ounce of cinnamon, an ounce of nutmeg, and two dozen cloves. They must all be ground or pounded to a fine powder, and thoroughly mixed. Keep the mixture in a bottle, labelled, and well corked. It will be found useful in seasoning many dishes; and being ready prepared will save much trouble. (A Book of Cookery by a Lady)

~~~~~~~~~~~~~~~~~~~~

Within an order to London, the Carroll's were looking for a good housekeeper. Charles describes her qualifications as follows — "we are in want of Sober orderly woman of a Good Character that understands Cooking Pickling Preserving and the other Requisites for a House keeper if Elderly we shall Like her the Better. I supposed such are to be met with that would on moderate wages I supposed about Ten or Twelve Pounds Sterling per Annum Come to a Good Place here for some years we shall be much obliged if such a one to be God that you would agree with Her for us on the best Terms and send her to us if above the ordinary Rank of servants my wife will Like her Better, as she will meet with all kind Treatment But she must not be of the flirting kind or one that give herself airs."

In September of 1768, Charles ordered a "Fashionable Genteel Larger Silver Waiter or Salver Seventeen or Eighteen inches in diameter or over, not thick Chased all over but a Genteel Light Sprig Round only and Coat of Arms in Middle." It was also described in more detail as to "Hold Eight or Ten Tea Cups and Saucers and is for a Tea Waiter. The small one is to stand in the middle of a Table to support a Dish as the Cross or X Lamps do not suit well must have a Genteel Cup or Pillar of Like the Glass stands used for Deserts. The Cups are for Drinking small Beer or Rhenish. Glasses are Continually Breaking."

In 1771, Margaret sailed with Charles to London for a visit per a letter that her father wrote to her, and wishes "every advantage and every enjoyment you may have in view." I can only imagine what they brought back with them and the experience they had there. It was supposed that she preferred her own home and the colonies to London. They also went to Bath so that Charles could take "the waters" due to his continual illness of "augue and fever." (History of Talbot County, Trostel) They returned on September 17, 1772 and it seems they had been gone for 18 months. The Maryland Gazette announced their return that day via the Nelly Frigate whose captain was Archibald Greig. On page two it says, "…in whom came Passengers Charles Carroll, Esq., of this City, Barrister, and his Lady."

Charles and Margaret are said to have had two children. Margaret was 37 when Margaret Clare was born on June 22, 1779. It is said that she was born at Mount Clare and baptized at St. Paul's Church in Baltimore on 6 December. There is no record of the birth, the name, or the baptism of the second child, but according to family tradition, there were twins. This really bothers me in that it would have been a joyful occasion after waiting 16 years to get pregnant, and there is no real record except in an 1840 memoir by Judge Nicholas Brice who was a great-nephew of the Barrister per Trostel's research. The Carroll's children did not survive, one died in April 1780, and then Margaret Clare in January 1781. They do not know where they are buried, but I cannot know the grief that Margaret would have had for her babies. I often wonder if the torn out pages of her account book recorded her children, and the grief had her cut them out. Being older in years, can we assume that there was some type of deformity or problem with them? We will never know unless there is mention in letters from relatives or friends that have not come to light.

In 1783, Charles died after catching a severe cold. Since he and Margaret had no surviving children, he bequeathed his land holdings, which included the property in Annapolis, to his nephews, Nicholas Maccubbin, Jr., and James Maccubbin, provided they change their family name to Carroll. He drew up his will shortly after Margaret Clare died. The Maryland Gazette documented the name change from Maccubbin to Carroll on June 5, 1783, following an official Act of Assembly in April of that year. (Maryland Historical Trust, inventory AA-1609)

It seems that Margaret took up full time residence at Mount Clare after Charles's death. She also entertained friends and visitors. One of the most important visitors, according to Robert Lewis's journal in 1789, was Martha Washington. She traveled through Baltimore to New York. She visited Mrs. Carroll at Mount Clare and the journal says, "Mrs. Carroll expecting Mrs. W had made considerable preparation, we found a large bowl of salubrious ice punch with fruits of which had been plucked from the trees in the Green House lying on the tables in great abundance, this after riding 25 to 30 miles without eating or drinking was no unwelcome luxury, however, Mrs. Carroll, could not complain that we had not done her punch honor, for in the course of 1 quarter of an hour (time we tarried this bowl which held upwards of two Gallons was entirely consumed to the no little satisfaction of us all –" Robert Lewis was the nephew and a secretary to George Washington.

General George Washington and Margaret wrote several letters back and forth between them, including the plans for an "orangerie," "green house," or "stove house" which Mrs. Carroll had at Mount Clare in which to grow her fruit trees as well as pineapples, aloe geraniums, among many other plants. On August 11, 1784, Washington wrote his former aide, Tench Tilghman, for the dimensions and other details of a greenhouse at Mrs. Margaret Tilghman Carroll's plantation in Maryland. Tilghman replied on August 18 sending details and sketches. (The George Washington Collection (Cadou) and GW Papers at the Library of Congress)

Washington continued correspondence in 1789 where Margaret had offered to send different plants and trees to him. He decided to take her up on the offer while he was in New York, on September 16, 1789, he writes —

"Mdam: A Person having been lately sent to me from Europe in the capacity of a Gardner, who professes a knowledge in the culture of rare plants and care of a Green-House, I am desirous to profit of the very obliging offer you were pleased some time ago to make me.

In availing myself of your goodness I am far from desiring that it should induce any inconvenience to yourself. but, reconciling your disposition to oblige, with your convenience, I shall be happy to receive such aids as you can well spare, and as will not impair your collection. Trusting that this will be the rule of your bounty, I have requested General Williams to give you notice, when an opportunity offers to transport the trees or plants in the freshest state to Mount Vernon, and to pay any expence which may be incurred in fitting them for transportation, and to receive them from your Gardner for that purpose. I have the honor etc."

Mrs. Carroll responded to this letter on September 25 assuring him that the "Trees shall be immediately put in order" and shipped as soon as Williams could procure a vessel.

"I have been rather unfortunate in the Shaddocks that were long intended for your Excellency's use, attempting to engraff on them my two other sorts of Fruit, have fail'd either for want of Skill in my Gardiner or that being an improper Stock for either of them, you will therefore please Sir to accept with them a Lemon Tree two yo[u]ng plants and a few Seedlings, those with two plants of the Aloe and a Geranium, which shall also be sent are all the kinds my Green-house affords and do not in the least disfurnish it. It will give me much pleasure to hear they get safe, and should they Succeed Shall think my Self happy having in the Smallest degree contributed to your convenience or amusement."

Margaret Tilghman Carroll

(MdHS, National Archives https://founders.archives.gov/documents/Washington/05-04-02-0025)

Mrs. Carroll's account book included a receipt for "Lemmon Cheesecakes" that included "Orange cheese cakes" within it. This receipt is verbatim to that in Eliza Smith's *The Compleat Housewife: Or, Accomplish'd Gentlewoman's Companion* dated 1739, printed in London by J & J Pemberton as well as in Hannah Glasse's *The Art of Cookery Made Plain and Easy,* dated 1788. In Hannah Glasse's copy — she includes a second cheesecake receipt that has egg whites and cream added. There are possibly other cookery books that have the same exact receipt.

~~~~~~~~~~~~~~~~~~~

Lemmon Cheesecakes

Take the peel of two large lemmons, boil it very tender, then pound it well in a mortar — with a ¼ lb of a loaf sugar — the yolks of six eggs — 3-1/2 pound of fresh butter — pound & mix all well together — & fill the pans but ½ full; **Orange cheese cakes** are done the same way; only you must boil the peel in two or three waters to take out the bitterness-."

So this receipt is fairly easy to make and does not, unless you make the orange cheese cakes, involve many steps. You can reduce the recipe by half or more. I would suggest that it be used as a topping on a cake versus eaten straight. It is extremely rich as the butter turns into more of a syrup after cooking. The original calls for 2 large lemons, ¼ pound (1/2 cup) of sugar, the yolks of 6 eggs, and 3-1/2 pounds (12 sticks) of butter. NOTE: I experimented with the receipt to cut it down even more than half and used 1 large lemon, 1/3 cup of sugar, 2 sticks of butter (1 cup), and 3 egg yolks so it wasn't too overwhelming to make. I diced the lemon peel instead of pulverizing it.

To get the lemons peels ready, you will need to boil them until tender, and then mash them into a mortar to essentially get the flavoring (I do not recommend skipping this step and using lemon juice, extract, or essence. Even if you boil the lemon and chop it fine — which I did — it will taste much better than an artificially produced extract).

In another bowl, beat the yolks of the eggs, add the sugar and mix, and then add the butter and cream it altogether. Then add your lemon. Fill small patty pans, either plain, fluted, or in shapes, and bake them in a slow oven (325 degrees) until done.

For the orange, you would need to boil the peels, take them off the fire/stove and drain. Do this three times and then pound them into your essence.

I must say that these were very buttery, and they tasted much better once cooled and refrigerated or put on ice.

~~~~~~~~~~~~~~~~~~~~

Margaret Tilghman Carroll

The General continued his correspondence with Margaret. He wrote on October 14, 1789, while in New York—

> "Madam: The letter with which you were pleased to honor me dated the 25. of last month, came duly to hand. I know not how sufficiently to thank you for your polite and obliging compliance with my request, nor, in what manner to express my fears lest those motives should have led you into inconveniences. My Green House is by no means in perfect order, and if it was, it would not have been my wish to have robbed yours of any *grown* or bearing plants. If it is not too late I would again repeat and entreat that this may not happen.
>
> Mrs. Washington joins me in thanking you for your polite invitation to Mount Clare (on the supposition that we should return to Virginia during the recess of Congress). For the more perfect reestablishment of my health among other considerations I am on the eve of a tour through the eastern States. We shall at all times have great pleasure in asking how you do and both of us unite in best wishes and respectful compliments. I have the honor etc." (GW Papers at the Library of Congress)

NOTE: On October 14, 1789 Washington also wrote to Otho Holland Williams, thanking him for his care and trouble in the matter of trees and plants from Mrs. Carroll, and requesting that if it was not too late, no large trees be sent "especially the one of which she has not a second. It is highly probable *this* tree, and perhaps *all* large ones would be lost to us both by the act of transportation unless very fine weather, a short passage, and *more* than *common* care are met with." (Maryland Historical Society)

Mrs. Carroll, however, wrote again on October 26 assuring Washington that—

"no inconvenience in the least, can arise, from the removal of the Trees. your Excellency rates them too highly, they will not be miss'd in my Green-house, nor will they be such an acquisition to yours, as I could wish; but it has been my intention, ever since I fail'd in buding the Shaddocks, to present you with them, if I could have a conveyance (for such) unfortunately General Williams has not yet procured me one; possibly your cautious Politenes may have prevented. yet mindfull of your Commands, and incapable of deviateing in the Smallest degree from them; he fears to remove, even a plant, without your permission, equally impres'd with a fear of incuring your disapprobation I am at a loss. how Sir shall I convince you, how much 'tis my inclination to furnish your Orangery with a little Fruit, and with what convenience I can do it, you shall judge, when I tell you, mine is rather over Stock'd. allow me then to send them, and I hope it will be pleaseing both to your Self and Mrs Washington to gather of your own fruit on your return.... Sensible of the inconvenience such a Correspondence must be to you, I can no longer trespass on your politeness, only be pleased to Say to General Williams that he may inform me when your Green-house is in order." (National Archives).

NOTE: A Shaddock is also known today as a Pomelo. It is a citrus fruit that is an ancestor to today's grapefruits. It would be perfect candied, dried, made into a jelly, marmalade, conserve, or syrup.

In a November 22, 1789 letter from George Washington to Margaret Carroll while he was in New York says —

"Madam: Since my return from a tour thro' the eastern States I have been honored by the receipt of your polite, and very obliging favor of the 26 of last month.

I am overcome by your goodness, and shall submit to your decision with respect to the plants from your Green House I must however again declare I should feel infinitely more pain than pleasure from the receipt of them, if I thought, in encreasing my stock, you had, in the smallest degree, done injury to your own. After this declaration, which I make, my good Madam, with the utmost candor and truth, such plants as your goodness may have intended for me, General Williams will forward when the season shall arrive, which will admit, with safety, of their transportation, and this from some late accounts of the alteration my new Gardner has been making at Mount Vernon will be as soon as my Green House will be completely in order for them.

I feel myself much flattered by your kind congratulations on the recovery of my health and the continuance of Mrs. Washington's and with gratitude I receive your obliging invitation to Mount Clare. Mrs. Washington joins me in compliments to you, and with very great respect, I have the honor etc." (GW Papers at the Library of Congress)

After Charles Carroll died in 1783, Margaret did not remarry. Margaret made changes to Mount Clare which included some architectural features that involved changing the circular window in the pediment of the house to a lunette-style window. She also had her portrait changed in 1788 to update the hair style so that she would be seen in the latest fashion, and had the spray of orange leaves in her right hand altered by having the oranges painted out. (Yamin) It is curious as to why she did this.

In 1812, her nephew Nicholas (Maccubbin) Carroll died, and as part of the settlement of the estate, Margaret was to receive an annuity during her life, in lieu of her thirds or dower right after Charles died, in certain of the real estate of Nicholas Carroll. (Maryland State Archives, Volume

618, p. 181). This allowed her to continue to live with an income to support her lifestyle.

Margaret Carroll died at Mount Clare on March 15, 1817 at the age of 75. Most of her estate was left to her nephew, Tench Peregrine Tilghman of Hope in Talbot County, with the rest divided among various family members. Her account book was given to her niece, Elizabeth Tench Goldsborough (who I suspect is the second style of hand writing within it) who called her, "Aunt Polly." Elizabeth listed those items left to her which included, as related to tea, a silver plate water urn, tea pot, two waiters, four goblets, a set of tea China blue and gold, one set tea China stencil'd, one old sugar dish, and one old cream pot, four cake dishes, four large tart pans, four small oval dishes with "pine apple edges," one dozen smallest sized punch cups, eight larger with fluted bottoms, eight decanters, three brandy bottles…

Postscript to the London Gazette

This "act of Parliament" was issued and printed, by authority in the London Gazette dated April 5, 1774, and reprinted in the South Carolina Gazette on June 3, 1774. It made it clear those in England were not happy with what happened in Boston, and that what happened only further enraged the colonists.

"PUBLISHED BY AUTHORITY.

THE following Act of Parliament, passed in the present Sessions, and which takes place on the First of JUNE next, is printed for the information of Merchants of Great-Britain and Ireland trading to North-America, viz. An Act to discontinue, in such manner and for such time as are therein mentioned, the landing and discharging, laaing or shipping of Goods, Wares, or Merchandize, at the Town, and within the Harbour of Buston, in the Province of Massichusetts-Bay, in North-America.

WHEREAS dangerous comotions and insurrections have been formented and raised in the town of Boston, in the province of Massachusetts Bay, in New-England, by divers ill-affected persons, to the subversion his Majesty's government, and to the utter destruction of the public peace and good

195

order of the said Town; in which commotions and insurrections certain valuable cargoes of Teas , being the property of the East-India Company, and on board certain vessels lying within the bay or harbour of Boston, were seized and destroyd: And whereas, in the present condition of the said town and harbour, the commerce of his Majesty's subjects cannot be safely carried on there, nor the customs payable to his Majesty duly collected; and it is therefore expedient that the Officers of his Majesty's Customs should be forthwith removed from the said Town: May it please your Majesty that it may be enacted; and be it enacted by the King's most excellent Majesty, by and with the consent of the Lords Spiritual and Temporal, and Commons, in this present Parliament assembled, and by the authority of the same, That from and after the first day of June. One thousand seven hundred and seventy-four, it shall not be lawful for any person or persons whatsoever, to lade or put, or cause to be laden and put, off or from any quay, wharf, or other place, within the said town of Boston, or in or upon any part of the shore of the bay, commonly called the harbour of Boston, between a certain headland or point called Nahant Point, on the Eastern side of the entrance into the said bay, and a certain other headland or point called Alderton Point, or the Western side of the entrance into the said bay, or in or upon any island, creek, landing place, bank, or other place, within the said bay or headlands, into any ship, vessel, lighter, boat, or bottom, any goods, wares, or merchandize whatsoever, to be transported or carried into any other country, province, or places whatsoever, or into any other part of the said province of the massachusetts Bay, in New-England; or to take up, charge, or lay on land, or cause or procure, to be taken up, discharged, or laid on land, within the said Town, or in or upon any of the laces aforesaid, out of any bat, lighter, ship, vessel, bottom, any goods, wares, or merchandize whatsoever, to be brought from any other country, province, or place, or any other part of the said province of the massachusetts Bay, in New-England, upon pain of the forfeiture of the said goods, wares, and merchandizes, and of the said boat, lighter, ship, vessel, or other bottom into which the same shall be put, or out of which the same shall be taken, and of guns, ammunition, tackle, furniture, and stores, in or belonging to the same: And if any such goods, wares, or merchandize, shall, within the said town, or in any of the places aforesaid, be laden or taken in from the shore into any barge, hoy, lighter, wherry, or boat, from or out of any ship or vessl coming in and arriving from any other country or province, or other part of the province of the Massachusetts Bay in New-England, such barge, hoy, lighter, wherry, or boat, shall be forfeited and lost.

And be it further enacted by the authority aforesaid, That if any wharfinger or keeper of any wharf, crane, or quay, or their servants, or any of them, shall take up or land, or knowingly suffer to be taken up or landed, or shall ship off, or suffer to be taken up or landed, or shall ship off, or suffer to be waterborne, at or from any of their said wharves, cranes, or quays, any such goods, wares, or merchandize; in every such case, all and every wharfinger, and keeper of such wharf, crane, or qusty, and every person whatsoever, who shall be assisting, or otherwise concerned in the shipping or in the loading or putting on board any boat, or other vessel, for that purpose, or in the unshipping such goods, wares, and merchandize, or to whose hands the same shall knowingly come after the loading, shipping, or unshipping thereof, shall forfeit and lose treble the value thereof, to be computed at the highest price which such sort of goods, wares, and merchandize, shall bear at the place where such offence shall be committed, at the time when the same shall be so committed, togethr with the vessels and boats, and all the horses, cartle, and carriages whatsoever, made use of in the shipping, unshipping, landing, removing, carriage, or conveyance of any of the said goods, wares, and merchandize.

And be it further enacted by the authority aforesaid, That if any ship of vessel shall be moored or lie at anchor, or be seen hovering within the said Bay, described and bounded as aforesaid, or within one league from the said Bay so described, or the said Headlands, or any of the islands lying between or within the same, it shall and may be lawful for any Admiral, Chief Commander, or commissioned Officer of his Majesty's fleet or ships of war, or for any Office of his Majesty's Customs, to compel such strip or vessel to depart to some other port or harbour, or to such station as the said Officer shall appoint, and to use such force for that purpose as shall be found necessary; And if such ship or vessel shall not depart accordingly, with six hours after notice for that part accordingly, within six hours after notice for that purpose given by such person as aforesaid, such ship or vessel together with all the goods laden on board thereon, and all the guns, ammunition, tackle, and furniture, shall be foreseited and lost, whether bulk shall have been broken or not.

Provided always. That nothing in this Act contained shall extend, or be construed to extend, to any military or other stores for his Majesty's use, or to the ships or vessels wherein the same shall be laden, which shall be commissioned by, and in the immediate pay of his Majesty, his being or successors, nor to any fuel or victuals brought coal-wise from any part of the continent of America, for the necessary use and sustenance of the inhabitants of the said town of Boston, provided the vessle wherein the same are to be carried shall be duty furnished with a cock-stand let-pass, after having been duty searched by the proper Officer of his Majesty's Customs at Marblehead, a port of Salem in the province of Massachusets Bay; and that some Officer, of his Majesty's by the proper Officer of his Majesty's Customs at Marblehead, in the port of Salem, in the province of Massacetts Bay; and that some Officer, of his Majesty's Customs be also there put on board the said vessel, who is hereby authorised to go on board, and proceed with the said vessel, together with a sufficient number of persons, properly armed, for his defense, to the said town or harbour of Boston; nor to any ships or vessels which may happen to be within the said harbour of Boston, on or before the first day of June, One thousand seven hundred and seventy-four, and may have either laden or taken on board, or be there with intent to load or take on board, or to land or discharge any goods, wares, and merchandize, provided the said ships and vessels do depart the said harbour within fourteen days after the said first day of June, One thousand seven hundred and seventy-four.

And be it further enacted by the authority aforesaid, That all seizures, penalties, and forfeitures, inflicted by this Act, shall be made and prosecuted by any Admiral, Chief Commander, or Commissioned Officer, of his Majesty's fleet, or ships of war, or by the Officers of his Majesty's Customs, or some of them, or by some other Person deputed or authorised, by warrant from the Lord High Treasurer, or the Commissioners of his Majesty's Treasury for the time being, and no other Person whatsoever: And if any such Officer, or other Person authorised as aforesaid, shall, directly or indirectly, take or receive any bribe or reward, to connive at such landing or unlanding, or shall make or commence any collusive seizure, information or agreement for the purpose, or shall do any other act whatsoever, whereby tthe goods, wares, or merchandize, prohibited as aforesaid, shall be suffered to pass either inwards or outwards, or whereby the forfeitures and penalties inflicted by this Act, may be evaded, every such offender shall forseit the sum of five hundred pounds for every such offence, and shall become incapable of any office or employment, civil or military; and every Person who shall give, offer, or promise, any such bribe or reward, or shall contract, agree, or treat any such offence, shall forfeit the sum of fifty pounds.

And be it further enacted by the authority aforesaid, That the forfeitures and penalties inflicted by this Act; shall and may be prosecuted, sued for, and recovered, and be divided, paid and applied, in like manner as other penalties and forfeitures, inflicted by any Act or Act of Parliament, relating to the trade or revenues of the British colonies of plantations in America, are directed to be prosecuted, sued for or recovered, divided, paid, and applied, by two several Acts of Parliament, the one passed in the fourth year of his present Majesty, intituled, An Act for granting certain duties in the British colonies and plantations in America; for continuing, amending, and making perpetual, an Act passed in the sixth year of the reign of his late Majesty King George the Second, intituled, AN Act for better securing and encouraging the trade of his Majesty's sugar, colonies in America; for applying the produce of such duties, "and the duties to arise by virtue of the aforesaid Act, towards defraying the expenses of protecting and securing the said colonies and plantations; for explaining an Act made in the twenty-fifth year of the reign of King Charles the Second, intituled, An Act for the encouragement of the Greenland and Eastland trades, and for the better securing the plantation trade; and for altering and disallowing several draw backs on exports from this kingdom, and more effectually preventing "the clandestine conveyance of goods to and from the said colonies and plantations, and improving and securing the trade between the same and Great-Britain; the other passed in the eighth year of his present Majesty's reign, intituled, An Act for the more easy and effectually recovery of the penalties and forfeitures inflicted by the Acts of Parliament relating to the trade or revenues of the British colonies and plantations in America.

And be it further enacted by the authority aforesaid. That every charter party, bill of loading, and other contract for consigning, shipping, or carrying any goods, wares, and merchandize whatsoever, to or from the said town of Boston, or any part of the bay or harbour thereof, described as aforesaid, which have been made or entered into, so long as this Act shall remain in full force, relating to any ship which shall arrive at the said town or harbour after the first day of June, One thousand seven hundred and seventy-four, shall be, and the same are hereby declared to be, utterly void, to all intents and purposes whatsoever.

And be it further enacted by the authority aforesaid, That whenever it shall be made to appear to his Majesty, in his Privy Council, that peace and obedience to the laws shall be so far restored in the said town of Boston, that the trade of Great-Britain may safely be carried on there, and his Majesty's customs duly collected, and his Majesty, in his Privy Council, shall adjudge that same to be the trade of Great-Britain may safely be carried on there, and his Majesty's customs duly collected, and his Majesty, in his Privy Council, shall adjudge that same to be true, it shall and may be lawful for his Majesty, by Proclamation, or order of Council, to assign and appoint the extent, bounds and limits, of the port or harbour of Boston, and of every creek or haven within the same, or in the islands within the precinct thereof: and also to assign and appoint such and so many open places, quays, and wharves, within the said harbour, creeks, havens, and islands, for the landing, discharging, lading and shipping of goods, as his Majesty, his heirs or successors, shall judge necessary and expedient; and also to appoint such and so many Officers of the customs therein as his Majesty shall think fit; after which it shall be lawful for any person or persons to lade or put off from, or to discharge and land upon, such wharfs, quays and places, so appointed within the said harbour, and none other, any goods, wares and merchandize whatever.

Provided always, That if any goods, wares or merchandize, shall be laden or put off from, or discharged or landed upon, any other place, than the quays, wharves or places, so to be appointed, the same, together with the ships, boats, and other vessels employed therein, and the horses, or other cattle and carriages used to convey the same, and the person or persons concerned or assisting therein, or to whose hands the same shall knowingly come shall suffer all the forfeitures and penalties imposed by this or any other Act on the illegal shipping or landing or goods.

Provided also, and it is hereby declared and enacted, That nothing herein contained shall extend, or be construed, to enable his Majesty to appoint such port harbour, creeks, quays, wharves, places, or officers, into the said town of Boston, or in the said bay or islands, until it shall sufficiently appear to his Majesty, that full satisfaction hath made by or on behalf of the inhabitants of the said town of Boston, to the United Company of Merchants of England trading to the East-Indies, for the damages sustained by the said Company, by the destruction of their goods sent to the town the Boston, on board certain ships or vessels as aforesaid; and until It shall be certified to his

Majesty, in Council, by the Governor or Lieutenant-Governor of the said Province, that reasonable satisfaction hath been made to the officers of his Majesty's revenue, and others, who suffered by the riots and insurrections above-mentioned, in the months of November and December, in the year One thousand seven hundred seventy-three, and in the month of January, in the year One thousand seven hundred and seventy-four.

And be it further enacted by the authority aforesaid, that if any action or suit shall be commenced, either in Great Britain or America, against any person or persons, for any thing done in pursuance of this Act of Parliament, the desendant or desendants, in such action or suit, may plead the general issue, and give the said act and the special matter in evidence, at any trial to be had thereupon, and that the same was done in pursuance and by the authority of this act; and if it shall appear so to have descendants; and if the Plaintiff shall be nonsuited, or discontinue his action, after the Desendant or Desendants shall have appeared; or if Judgment shall be given upon any Verdict or Demurrer, against the Plaintiff, the Defendant or Defendants shall recover treble Costs, and have the like remedy for the same, as Defendants have in other cases by Law."

Postscript to the Pennsylvania Gazette

On a Friday Evening at Five 'Clock, December 24, 1773 within Philadelphia...

"At Two o'Clock this Afternoon arrived in this City a Gentleman, who came Express from New York, with the following interesting Advices from BOSTON, which were sent there by Express also.

BOSTON, December 16.
IT being understood that Mr. Rotch, owner of the ship Dartmouth, rather lingered in his preparations to return her to London, with the East India Company tea on board, there was on Monday last, P. M. a meeting of the Committee of several of the neighbouring towns in Boston, and Mr. Rotch was sent for, and enquired of, whether he continued his resolution to comply with the injunctions of the body, assembled at the Old South Meeting house on Monday and Tuesday preceding. Mr. Rotch answered, that in the interim he had taken the advice of the best council, and found that in case he went on of his own motion, to send that ship to sea, in the condition she was

then in, it must inevitably ruin him, and therefore he must beg them to consider that he had said at the said meeting, to be the effect of compulsion and unadvised, and in consequence that he was not holden to abide by it, when he was now assured that he must be utterly ruined in case he did. Mr. Rotch was then asked whether he would demand a clearance for his ship in the Custom House, and in case of a refusal enter a protest, and then apply in like manner for a pass, and order her to sea? to all which he answered in the negative: The Committees, doubtless, informing their respective constituents of what had passed, a very full meeting of the body was again assembled at the Old South Meeting house on Tuesday afternoon, and Mr. Rotch, being again present, was enquired of as before, and a motion was made and seconded, that Mr. Rotch be enjoined forthwith to repair to the Collector of the Customs, and demand a clearance for his ship, and ten gentlemen were appointed to accompany him, as witnesses of the demand. Mr. Rotch then proceeded with the Committee to Mr. Harrison lodgings, and made the demand. Mr. Harrison observed, he could not give answer, till he consulted the Comptroller, but would, at office hours next morning, give a decisive answer. On the return of Mr. Rotch and the Committee to the body with this report, the meeting was adjourned to Thursday morning at 10 o'clock.

THURSDAY.
Having met on Thursday morning, 10 o'clock, they sent for Mr. Rotch, and asked him, if he had been to the Collector, and demanded a clearance? he said he had; but the Collector said, that he could not, consistent with his duty, give him a clearance, till all the dutiable articles were out of his ship; they then demanded of him, whether he had protested against the

Collector? he said he had not: They ordered him, upon his peril, to give immediate orders to the Captain, to get his ship ready for sea that day, enter a protest immediately against the Custom House, and then proceed directly to the Governor (who was at his seat at Milton, 7 miles off) and demand a pass for his ship to go by the castle. They then adjourned to 3 o'clock, P. M. to wait Mr. Rotch return; having met according to adjournment, there was the fullest meeting ever known (it was reckoned, that there were 2000 men from the country) they waited very patiently till about 5 o'clock, when they found Mr. Rotch did not return, they began to be very uneasy, called for a dissolution of the meeting, and finally obtained a vote for it: But the more moderate part of the meeting, fearing what would be the consequences, begged that they would reconsider their vote, and wait till Mr. Rotch return, for this reason, that they ought to do every thing in their power to send the tea back, according to their resolves.

They obtained a vote, to remain together one hour longer; in about three quarters of an hour, Mr. Rotch returned; his answer from the Governor was, that he could not give a pass, till the ship was cleared by the Custom House; the people immediately, as with one voice, called for a dissolution, which having obtained, they repaired to Griffin wharff, where the tea vessels lay, proceeded to fix tackles, and hoisted the tea upon deck, cut the chests to pieces, and threw the tea over the side; there were two ships and a brig, Captains Hall, Bruce and Coffin, each vessel having 114 chests of tea on board; they began upon the two ships first, as they had nothing on board but the tea, then proceeded to the brig, which had hawled to the wharff but the day before, and had but a small part of her cargoe out. The Captain of the brig begged they would not begin with his vessel, as the tea was covered with goods, belonging to different Merchants in town. They told him the tea they wanted, and the tea they would have; but if he would go into his cabin quietly, not one article of his goods should be hurt. They immediately proceeded to remove the goods, and then to dispose of the tea.

It was expected that the men of war would have interfered, as all the Captains and other officers were ordered on board their ships before night; and the day before, there were six dozen of lanterns sent on board the Admiralship. The King Fisher, and several armed schooners, were rigged and fitted for sea, and the Gaspee armed brig arrived that day from Rhode Island. The people were determined. It is to be observed, that they were extremely careful, that not any of the tea should be stolen, so kept a good look out, and detected one man filling his pockets, whom they treated very roughly, by tearing his coat off his back, and driving him up the wharff, through thousands of people, who cuffed and kicked him as he passed.

We are positively informed, that the patriotic inhabitants of Lexington, at a late meeting, unanimously resolved against the use of Bohea tea of all sorts, Dutch or English importation; and to manifest the sincerity of their resolution, they brought together every ounce contained in the town, and committed it to one common bonfire.

We are also informed, Charlestown is in motion to follow their illustrious example.

Quere. Would it not materially affect the bringing this detestable herb into disuse, if every town would enjoin their Selectmen to deny licences to all houses of entertainment, who were known to afford tea to their guests?

Our reason for suggesting this is, the difficulty these people are under to avoid dishing out this poison, without such a provision in their favour.

We have this moment received intelligence, that Mr. Clarke brigantine, commanded by Captain Loring, bilged at the back of Cape Cod. The Captain has not landed his tea there, of which he has 58 chests on board, belonging to the East India Company.

*By the act, any dutiable goods on board a vessel, after lying 20 days in a harbour, become liable to the payment of the duties. The people waited till the last day, and in a few hours the ship (to secure the duties then payable) was to have been delivered to the custody of the man of war.

NEW YORK, December 22.
Last night an express arrived here from Boston, who left it on Friday last, and brings sundry letters, among which is the following, viz.

GENTLEMEN, *Boston, Dec. 17, 1773.*
YESTERDAY we had a greater Meeting of the Body than ever, the Country coming in from 20 Miles round, and every Step was taken that was practicable for returning the Teas. The Moment it was known out of Doors, that Mr. Rotch could not obtain a Pass for his Ship by the Castle, a Number of People huzza in the Street, and in a very little Time, every Ounce of the Teas on board of Captains Hall, Bruce and Coffin, was immersed in the Bay, without the least injury to private Property. "The Spirit of the People on this Occasion, surprized all Parties, who view the Scene.

"We conceived it our Duty to afford you the [ ] Advice of this interesting Event by Express, which, departing immediately, obliges us to conclude.

[Signed] By Order of the Committee.

P.S. The other Vessel, viz. Captain Loring, belonging to Messrs. Clark, with Fifty eight Chests, was, by the Act of God, cast on Shore, on the Back of Cape Cod."

Paintings/Illustrations

Cover — "Teapot and Violet" by Pamela Patrick White of White Historic Art

College Breakfast, J. Nixon invt. et fecit ; Robt. Laurie sculpsit, 1783 Courtesy of the Lewis Walpole Digital Library, Yale University

The Tea Table, Courtesy of the Lewis Walpole Collection, Yale University

Benjamin Harbeson at the Golden Tea Kettle, 1776, Winterthur

Joseph Badger (1708-1755) American MRS. NATHANIEL LORING (MARY GYLES), c. 1760-63, Oil on canvas, 50 x 39 inches (127 x 99 cm), The Dayton Art Institute, Gift of Sam and Selma Maimon and the Maimon Family, 2002.11

A Harlot's Progress, Plate 3, The Harlot at Her Dwelling in Drury Lane, Winterthur Museum item number 1985.0156.001

Mrs. Margaret Tilghman Carroll, Mount Clare Museum House, Baltimore, Maryland

Paintings/Illustrations

Photographs taken by Kimberly K. Walters and Kenneth Tom, volunteer with Historic Annapolis

Henry Miller at the Tea Store, Baltimore, Receipt Museum Object #1952.0029, Winterthur

Acknowledgements

TO my Mom and Dad. No other words are needed to know the love they had for me. They were my inspiration, and they let me know that I could do anything I set my mind to. I cannot thank them enough for their support to me, and teaching me all they could. So many lessons learned, and values given to me. I miss them every single day.

TO Jim McGaughey for the idea to write another book, for his encouragement and patience. He continues to always make me laugh and I value him in my life.

TO Lucinda Brant for her support and encouragement. I am honored that she took the time to read through my manuscript and write the foreward to this book. We have worked on a couple of projects together, and I cannot thank her enough for all of her support. Her own books were ones that I could not put down, and I cannot wait to read more! Her website is www.lucindabrant.com

TO Sue Freivald who took the time to help me with this book from encouragement to suggested edits. I am blessed to have her as my friend as we share our love for our horses.

Acknowledgements

TO Rodris Roth, author of *Tea Drinking in the 18th Century it's Etiquette and Equipage* for her research and writing about tea before the internet made it much easier.

TO Kerry McClure, the epitome of the 18th century lady living in the 21st century. I was honored to serve tea to her at Patrick Henry's Scotchtown, and am grateful for her modeling for this book. Her encouragement and support to me has been invaluable. She is also one of my very best friends.

TO Catherine Curzon for her encouragement and support in writing another book. I am thankful to her for believing in me. Her website is www.madamgilflurt.com

TO Pamela Patrick White for allowing me to use another of her amazing paintings as the cover art. I appreciate her support to me in all I do as well as loving to paint horses, including my Nelson before and after he became mine, which is one of my favorite subjects! You can see more of her paintings at www.whitehistoricart.com

TO Jamison Borek for all of her help providing assistance with research, and her encouragement in all that I do. Her support and collaboration has been invaluable. www.shrewsburypress.com

A huge thank you to Harry Aycock for helping me with the Annapolis-based research, continued discussions on family connections, imports into the colonies, and for being a good friend to me.

TO Chris Washack of Hemlock Hollow Floorcloths for making the floor cloth used at Patrick Henry's Scotchtown of which is included in a photo in this book. www.hemlockhollowfloorcloths.net

ANOTHER huge thank you to Gema Gonzalez who is one of the most gracious women that I have ever met. I truly appreciate her allowing me to use her image in my book, and for her continued wonderful and true friendship.

TO Connie Unangst for assisting me with receipt research and our realizing that Mrs. Carroll's account book copied verbatim some receipts from cookery books of the day — as if she was writing those she wanted to remember without having to look them up again (that sounds familiar and just like my Book of Cookery by a Lady — my first book).

TO Robin Marchionni for assisting me as a test cook, for her support, and valued friendship.

TO Zachary Long for agreeing to help as a test cook, and for going the extra mile and cooking original receipts from Mrs. Carroll's account book in the Daniel Boone Homestead hearth kitchen. Huzzah!

A huge thank you to Dr. Lynn Price for her expertise in all things Martha Washington, as well as for her friendship. (http://gwpapers.virginia.edu/martha-washington-papers-project/)

About the Author

Kimberly K. Walters is a living historian that started reenacting as a hearth cook in 2009 as the Washington Headquarters housekeeper modeled after Mrs. Elizabeth Thompson. Her book, *A Book of Cookery by a Lady*, was a tribute to Mrs. Thompson, and published in 2014 on what would have been Kim's mother's birthday. An acknowledgement to her special day.

Kim has participated in living history events independently or as a part of the British Brigade and Continental Line reenactment units at various historic sites up and down the East Coast of the United States.

She cooks at historic sites and in camp with reenactment units she belongs to. Kim eventually started a hearth cooking guild where she practiced her skills, taught those who wanted to also learn, and now cooks upon request at various sites.

Kim is an avid horse woman, animal lover, and historian. She is currently a member of the Fincastle Chapter of Louisville, Kentucky of the National Society Daughters of the American Revolution. She is the sole proprietor of K. Walters at the Sign of the Gray Horse where she creates and sells reproduction and historically inspired jewelry to care for her rescued and Colonial Williamsburg retired horses.

Bibliography

A Collection of Above Three Hundred Receipts in Cookery, Physick, and Surgery: For the Use of All Good Wives, Tender Mothers, and Careful Nurses, 1714.

Ash, John, *The New and Complete Dictionary of the English Language*, Edward and Charles Dilly...and R. Baldwin, 1775, original from the New York Public Library, Digitized March 3, 2009, Google Books.

Berkeley, Jr., Edmund, *The Diary, Correspondence, and Papers of Robert King Carter of Virginia, 1701-1732*. http://carter.lib.virginia.edu//.

Borella, Mr., *The Court and Country Confectioner: Or, The House-keeper's Guide; to a More Speedy, Plain, and Familiar Method of Understanding the Whole Art of Confectionary, Pastry, Distilling, and the Making of Fine Flavoured English Wines from All Kinds of Fruits, Herbs, and Flowers* ...G. Riley and A. Cooke, 1770.

Branch, E. Douglas, *Notes and Documents, Henry Bouquet: His Relict Possessions*, Western Pennsylvania Historical Magazine, Volume 22, page 201-208, 1939.

British Library On-Line, *China Trade and the East India Company, China Trade.* http://www.bl.uk/reshelp/findhelpregion/asia/china/guidesources/chinatrade.

Byrd, William, *Diary of William Byrd II of Virginia 1709-1712*, ed. Louis B. Wright and Marion Tinling, Richmond: The Dietz Press, 1941. http://nationalhumanitiescenter.org/pds/becomingamer/economies/text5/williambyrddiary.pdf.

Carson, Jane, *Colonial Virginia Cookery: Procedures, Equipment, and Ingredients in Colonial Cooking*, Colonial Williamsburg Foundation: Williamsburg VA, 1985.

Carroll, Margaret, 1742-1817, "Account Book 1815-1817," Special Collections, Maryland Historical Society.

Carlyle John, Inventory of Colo. John Carlyles Estate Real & Personal taken 13th Novmr. 1780, Fairfax County Will Book D-1, 1777-1783, p. 368-394.

Chastellux, Marquis de, *Voyages de M. le Marquis de Chastellux dans l'Amerique Septentriomale*, Paris, 1788.

Chippendale, Thomas, *The gentleman and cabinet-maker's director: being a large collection of the most elegant and useful designs of household furniture in the Gothic, Chinese and modern taste*, 1754, Digital Library for the Decorative Arts and Material Culture, University of Wisconsin Digital Collections Center. http://digicoll.library.wisc.edu/cgi-bin/DLDecArts/DLDecArts-idx?type=header&id=DLDecArts.ChippGentCab&isize=M&pview=hide.

Dillard, Richard. *The Historic Tea-Party of Edenton, October 25th, 1774. An Incident in North Carolina Connected with British Taxation.* Edenton, NC: N.P, 1898. https://archive.org/details/historicteaparty01dill.

Domestic Management, or the Art of Conducting a Family; with Instructions to Servants in General Addressed to Young Housekeepers, London, H.D. Symonds, at the Literary Press, No 62, Wardour-Street, Soho, Circa 1800, Original British Museum, taken from Google Books. https://books.google.com/books?id=FrJcAAAAcAAJ&printsec=frontcover&source=gbs_ge_summary_r&cad=0#v=onepage&q&f=false.

Eddis, William, *Letters from America, Historical and Descriptive Comprising Occurrences* from 1769 to 1777, Inclusive, London, Printed for the Author, 1792.

Fitzpatrick, John C., ed. The Writings of Washington from the Original Manuscript Sources, 1745-1799, 39 vols. Washington, DC: Government Printing Office, 1931-1944.

Fitzpatrick, John C., ed. George Washington's Accounts of Expenses While Commander-in-Chief of the Continental Army, 1775-1783. Boston: Houghton Mifflin Company, 1917.

From George Washington to Margaret Tilghman Carroll, 16 September 1789," Founders Online, National Archives, last modified December 28, 2016, http://founders.archives.gov/documents/Washington/05-04-02-0025. [Original source: *The Papers of George Washington*, Presidential Series, vol. 4, *8 September 1789–15 January 1790*, ed. Dorothy Twohig. Charlottesville: University Press of Virginia, 1993, pp. 43–47.]

Bibliography

"To George Washington from William Heth, 3 May 1789," *Founders Online,* National Archives, last modified December 28, 2016, http://founders.archives.gov/documents/Washington/05-02-02-0146. [Original source: *The Papers of George Washington,* Presidential Series, vol. 2, *1 April 1789–15 June 1789,* ed. Dorothy Twohig. Charlottesville: University Press of Virginia, 1987, pp. 204–206.]

Glasse, Hannah, *The Compleat Confectioner, Or The Whole Art of Confectionary Made Plain and Easy, Etc,* J. Cooke, 1765.

Glasse Hannah, *The Art of Cookery Made Plain and Easy, by a Lady,* J. Rivington and Sons, 1788.

Glasse, Hannah, "The Art of Cookery Made Plain and Easy," London, 1774 (own original). Goose Bay Workshops, www.goosebay-workshops.com, makes a lovely sabotiere for those interested.

Harrison, Sarah and Mary Morris, *The House-keeper's Pocket-book, and Compleat Family Cook: Containing Above Twelve Hundred Curious and Uncommon Receipts in Cookery, Pastry, Preserving, Pickling, Candying, Collaring, &c., with Plain and Easy Instructions for Preparing and Dressing Every Thing Suitable for an Elegant Entertainment, from Two Dishes to Five Or Ten, &c., and Directions for Ranging Them in Their Proper Order,* 1760

Higgenbotham, Don, *The Papers of James Iredell,* Volume I, 1767-1777, North Carolina State Library, Raleigh, 1976.

The Tea Act. http://www.ushistory.org/declaration/related/teaact.html.

Jeremy, David John, "Henry Wansey and His American Journal 1794," American Philosophical Society, 1970, p. 99-100.

Jarrin, William Alexis, *Italian Confectioner; Or, Complete Economy of Desserts, According to the Most Modern and Approved Practice*, John Ebers and Company, 1829.

Kalm, Peter (Pehr), *Travels Into North America: Containing Its Natural History… with the Civil, Ecclesiastical and Commercial State of the Country…* Eyres, 1771.

Leslie, Eliza, *Directions for Cookery, in its Various Branches*, Philadelphia: E. L. Carey & A. Hart. 1840.

Lewis, Robert, 1769-1829, *Journal of a Journey from Fredericksburg, Virginia to New York 13-20 May 1789*, 1789-1805, Robert Lewis Manuscripts, Digital Collections from the Washington Library Maryland State Archives, Chancery Court (Chancery Papers, Exhibits) Wallace, Davidson Johnson, Order Books, 1771/4/25-1775/11/16. MSA S 528-27/28.

Menon, The French Family Cook: Being a System of French Cookery, J. Belle, 1793.

Moreno, Kimberly *"Mistress of Mount Clare: The Life of Margaret Tilghman Carroll 1742-1817,"* Masters Thesis, University of Maryland Baltimore County, 2004.

Myers, Albert Cook, *Sally Wister's Journal: a true narrative; being a Quaker maiden's account of her experiences with officers of the Continental Army, 1777-1778*, Ferris & Leach, Philadelphia, Pennsylvania, 1902.

Nott, John, The Cooks and Confectioners Dictionary; or, The Accomplish'd Housewifes Companion, C. Rivington, 1723.

Bibliography

Parkinson, The Complete Confectioner, Pastry-cook, and Baker: Plain and Practical Directions for Making Confectionary and Pastry, and for Baking..., J.B. Lippincott and Co., 1864.

Pettigrew, Jane and Richardson, Bruce, *A Social History of Tea, Tea's Influence on Commerce, Culture & Community*, Benjamin Press, 2014.

Pierre Pomet, *Histoire generale des drogues, traitant des plantes, des animaux, & des mineraux*, Paris: Loyson & Pillon, 1694 (General History of Drugs: dealing with plants, animals, and minerals: workbook of over four hundred figures in Italian). (Google Books Project.)

Pitton de Tournefort, Joseph Materia Medica; or, a description of simple medicines generally us'd in physick: ... demonstrating their uses, ... also their operating ... upon human bodies ... With an appendix, shewing the nature and use of mineral waters ... Translated into English. The second edition, London 1716. (Google Books Project.)

Priest, William, *Commencing in the Year 1793, and Ending in 1797. With The Author's Journals of his Two Voyages Across the Atlantic*; London: Printed for J. Johnson, No. 72, St. Paul's Church-Yard, 1802, Bryer, Printer, Bridewell Hospital, Bridge Street.

Randolph, Mrs. Mary, *The Virginia Housewife: Or, Methodical Cook*, Baltimore: Plaskitt, & Cugle. 1838.

Raffald, Elizabeth, *The Experienced English Housekeeper: For the Use and Ease of Ladies, Housekeepers, Cooks, &c.: Written Purely from Practice: Consisting of Several Hundred Original Receipts, Most of which Never Appeared in Print*...A. Millar, W. Law, and R. Carter, 1788.

Roberts, Kenneth and Anne M., *Moreau de St. Mery's American Journey* [1793-1798], Doubleday & Company, Inc., Garden City, New York, 1947.

Rosen, Diana, *Teas of Yore, Bohea, Hyson, and Congou*, Tea Muse, October 1, 2003. http://www.teamuse.com/article_031001.html.

Roth, Rodris, "Tea Drinking in 18th-Century America: Its Etiquette and Equipage," United States National Museum, Smithsonian Institution, Washington, D.C. 1961 (own original).

Rundell, Maria Eliza Ketelby, *A New System of Domestic Cookery*, Philadelphia: Benjamin C. Buzby, 1807.

Ruschenberger, William Samuel Waithman, *A Voyage Round the World during the Years 1835, 1836, 1837…*, Richard Bentley, London, 1838.

Sherill, Charles H., French Memoraies of Eightenth-Century America, New York 1915. Marquis de Chastellux, Voyages de M. le Marquis de Chastellux dans l'Amerique Septentriomale, Paris 1788.

Shelley, Henry C., *Inns and Taverns of Old London*, L. C. Page & Company, Boston, Massachusetts, 1909.

Simmons, Amelia, *American Cookery*, Applewood Books, 1996.

Timbs, John, *Club Life of London with Anecdotes of the Clubs, Coffee-Houses and Taverns of the Metropolis During the 17th, 18th, and 19th Centuries*, Volume 2, Richard Bentley, 1866.

The Papers of George Washington Digital Edition, ed. Theodore J. Crackel. Charlottesville: University of Virginia Press, Rotunda, 2008. Canonic URL: http://rotunda.upress.virginia.edu/founders/GEWN-03-05-02-0133

[accessed 20 Jan 2012]. Original source: Revolutionary War Series (16 June 1775–14 January 1779), Volume 5.

The Whole Duty of a Woman Or, An Infallible Guide to the Fair Sex: Containing Rules, Directions, and Observations, for Their Conduct and Behavior Through All Ages and Circumstances of Life, as Virgins, Wives, Or Widows: with ... Rules and Receipts in Every Kind of Cookery, 1737.

Trostel Michael F., "*Mount Clare, Being an Account of the Seat built by Charles Carroll, Barrister, upon his Lands at Patapsco,*" National Society of Colonial Dames of America in the State of Maryland, 1981.

Van Braam, Authentic Account, 1:viii-ix; "Library Company Annual Report," 44

Walters, Kimberly K., *A Book of Cookery by a Lady Containing Above Three Hundred Receipts Made at Hearth, Suitable for an Elegant Entertainment or Common Fare for Preparing and Dressing Every Thing Suitable for Drinking and Dining at Any Time of the Day including Receipt for Lent, Household Cleaning, and Remedies for Ailments*, Ingram, 2014.

Yamin, Rebecca and Metheny Karen Bescherer, Landscape Archeaology: Reading and Interpreting the American Historical Landscape, University of Tennessee Press, 1996.

Index of Recipes

A Biscuit Cake   98
A Cake Rolled Up in the Form of' a
    Snail   109
A Common Seed Cake   108
A Cream Tart   139
A Dish of Snow   128
A Floating Island   122
A Good Plain bun, that may be eaten
    with or without toasting and
    butter   100
Almond Cakes   130
Almond Custards   143
Almond Pye   145
A Method to Make all Sorts of Light,
    Seed, and other Cakes   108
A Nice Kind of Breakfast Cake   90
Another Sort   98
Another sort, as Biscuits   97
Another Way...   145
Apple Butter   104
Apple Fritters   147
A Puff Paste for Tarts or Pyes with
    Fruit, Preserves, and Other
    Sweet Meats   125
A Refreshing Drink in a Fever   84
A Sally Lunn   93
A Tart with a Marmalade of
    Apples   136

A White Currant Cake   108
Baked Apples   104
Barberry Pastils   147
Beef Tea   86
Benton Tea Cakes   97
Bitter Almond Bomboons   147
Bloomage   126
Bol Ammoniac   174
Buckwheat Cakes   88
Carmine   171
Chocolate Pastils   110
Clouted Cream   103
Coffee Conserves (Chocolate)   143
Colours Good to Eat   170
Common Muffins   92
Common Rolls   96
Compotes of Cherries   123
Cracknels   99
Crack Nuts   99
Cream Cakes   95
Currant Ices   140
Directions for making of Fruit
    Jellies   133
Directions For The Ices Made With
    Preserved Fruits   107
Dry Cherries In Bunches   131
Eggs   84
Fallel Cakes   89

225

For a Cough   85
For the Gout   84
For the Rheumatism   85
For the Rheumatism   85
French Rolls   96
Gamboge   173
Green Gages   122
How to Keep Fruit for Tarts all the Year   102
How to Make Naples Biscuit   94
Ice Cream   115
Indian Batter Cakes   90
Indian Flappers   91
Indian Muffins   91
Indian Mush Cakes   90
Isinglass Jelly   105
Ivory Black   174
Johnny Cake   91
Kitchen Pepper (Another Way)   185
Lemmon Cheesecakes   190
Lemon Cream   139
Lemon or Orange Bomboons   144
Light Cake   87
Light Light Whipt Syllabubs   134
Macaroons   98
Marmalade of Apples or Pears   135
Moist Ananas Or Pine Apples   121
Moist Angelica   138
Moist Peaches   123
Muffin Bread   182
Nonpareils   119
Observations On Ices, Made With Ripe Fruits   136
Of Decoration   175
Of Pieces Montees   177
Of Preparing Cochineal   171
Of Strawberries and Iced Creams   116
Of Using Colours   175
On the Construction of Assiettes and Pieces Monties   175
Orange or Lemon Tart   132
Peach Cordial   183
Plumb Tart   148
Prussian Blue   174

Receipt for the Gout and Rheumatism   86
Rice Cakes   95
Richer Buns   100
Royal Cream Ices   137
Royal Paste   124
Saffron   173
Sage Tea   83
Salmon in Cases   111
Sap Green   174
Short Cakes   93
Soda Biscuits   93
Spinach Green   174
Strawberry Fritters   147
Sugared Figs   140
Sugared Grapes   138
Sugar Pears   127
Sword Knots   124
Tea Biscuits   94
Tea Cakes   96, 97
Tea Caudle   83
Tea Cream   103
Tea Cream Ices   107
Tea Custard   87
The Best Receipt for Ginger Bread   87
The Floating Island   117
The Way To Mould Ices In All Sorts Of Fruits   106
To Broil Salmon   110
To Choose Cochineal   171
To Colour Jellies   105
To Colour Nonpareils   119
To Cure the Flux   86
To keep Grapes, Gooseberries, Apricots, Peaches, Nectarines, Cherries, Currants, and Plumbs, the Whole Year   117
To keep Wallnuts, or Filberds, all the year   117
To Keep Walnuts All The Year Moist   120
To Make a Bread and Butter Puddings   102
To Make A Fine Saffron Cake   109

Index of Recipes

To Make A Hartshorn Flummery   134
To Make a Trifle   143
To Make Black Caps   128
To Make Brown Wafer   100
To Make Clotted Cream   103
To Make Fine Syllabubs   134
To Make Green Caps   128
To make Gum Cakes   131
To Make Lemon, Orange, And
    Flower Cakes   130
To Make Minced Meat   141
To Make Minced Pies For Lent   142
To Make Mince Pies Another Way   141
To make Naples Biscuits   146
To Make Quadrille Cards   135
To make Savoy Biscuits   145
To make Sponge Biscuits   146
To Make Tarts   101
To Make Tea Crumpets   88
To Pickle Walnuts Black   139
To Preserve Walnuts White   120
To Stew Pears Purple   118
Transparent Marmalade   137
Vegetable Carmine   172
Violet Cakes   131
Wafers   98
Water Muffins   92
White Lemon Conserves   144
Whole Currants   142
Whole Strawberries   133

CPSIA information can be obtained
at www.ICGtesting.com
Printed in the USA
BVHW011811280420
578732BV00006B/20/J